P9-DOG-531

The Ideals Classic Christmas Treasury

Christmas is coming,
the goose is getting fat,
Please to put a penny in
the old man's hat;
If you haven't got a penny,
a ha'penny will do,
If you haven't got a ha'penny,
then God bless you!

Beggar's Rhyme

IDEALS PUBLICATIONS INCORPORATED
NASHVILLE, TENNESSEE

ACKNOWLEDGMENTS

CHRISTMAS DAY IN THE MORNING by Pearl S. Buck. Reprinted by permission of Harold Ober Associates Incorporated. Copyright © 1955 by Pearl S. Buck. MY CHRISTMAS MIRACLE by Taylor Caldwell. Reprinted by permission of the William Morris Agency, Inc. on behalf of the Author. Copyright © 1961 by Taylor Caldwell; Copyright renewed 1983; LETTER FROM SANTA CLAUS from MY FATHER, MARK TWAIN by Clara Clemens. Copyright © 1931 by Clara Clemens Gabrilowitsch, renewed © 1958 by Clara Clemens Samossoud. Reprinted by permission of HarperCollins Publishers, Inc.; A CHRISTMAS CAROL by G.K. Chesterton. Copyright © by A.P. Watt Limited. Reprinted in North America by permission of Georges Borchardt, Inc. in conjunction with A.P.Watt Limited; THE OLD AMAZE (18 lines) from THIS GOLDEN SUMMIT by GRACE NOLL CROWELL. Copyright 1937 by Harper & Brothers. Copyright renewed 1964 by GRACE NOLL CROWELL. Reprinted by permission of HarperCollins Publishers, Inc.; CHRISTMAS TREES by Robert Frost, edited by Edward Connery Lathem. Copyright © 1916 and 1969 by Holt, Rinehart and Winston. Copyright © 1944 by Robert Frost. Reprinted by permission of Henry Holt and Co., Inc.; ANGELS by Billy Graham, Copyright 1975, Word Publishing, Dallas, Texas. All rights reserved; GOING HOME FOR CHRISTMAS and SANTA IS COMING by Edgar A. Guest. Used by permission of the author's estate; LET'S KEEP CHRISTMAS by Peter Marshall. Reprinted by permission of Chosen Books, a division of Baker Book House Company. Copyright © 1952, 1953. Copyright renewed 1981 by Catherine Marshall; ALL THE DAYS OF CHRISTMAS by Phyllis McGinley from MERRY CHRISTMAS , HAPPY NEW YEAR; Reprinted by permission of Curtis Brown, Ltd.; Copyright © 1958 by Phyllis McGinley; THE BALLAD OF THE HARP-WEAVER by Edna St. Vincent Millay. From COLLECTED POEMS, HarperCollins. © 1923, 1951 by Edna St. Vincent Millay and Norma Millay Ellis. Reprinted by permission of Elizabeth Barnett, literary executor. A GIFT OF THE HEART by Norman Vincent Peale. Reprinted with permission from the January 1968 Reader's Digest. Copyright © 1967 by The Reader's Digest Assn., Inc.; A CHRISTMAS STORY by Katherine Anne Porter; From A CHRISTMAS STORY by Katherine Anne Porter and illustrated by Ben Shahn. Copyright 1946, 1967 by Katherine Anne Porter, illustration © 1961 by Ben Shahn; Used by permission of Dell Books, a division of Bantam Doubleday Dell Publishing Group, Inc.; Our sincere thanks to the following authors whom we were unable to contact: E.C. Baird for I AM THE CHRISTMAS SPIRIT; Clarence Hawkes for THE CHRISTMAS GUEST; and T.F. Powys for A CHRISTMAS GIFT.

Cover Painting:
DECORATING THE CHRISTMAS TREE, watercolor on masonite by Richard Hook

ISBN 0-8249-4064-4

Printed and bound in the United States of America

Published by Ideals Publications Incorporated
565 Marriott Drive
Nashville, TN 37214

Film separations by Precision Color Graphics, New Berlin, WI
Printed and Bound by R.R. Donnelly, Willard, Ohio

Contents

Christmas Is for Anticipation

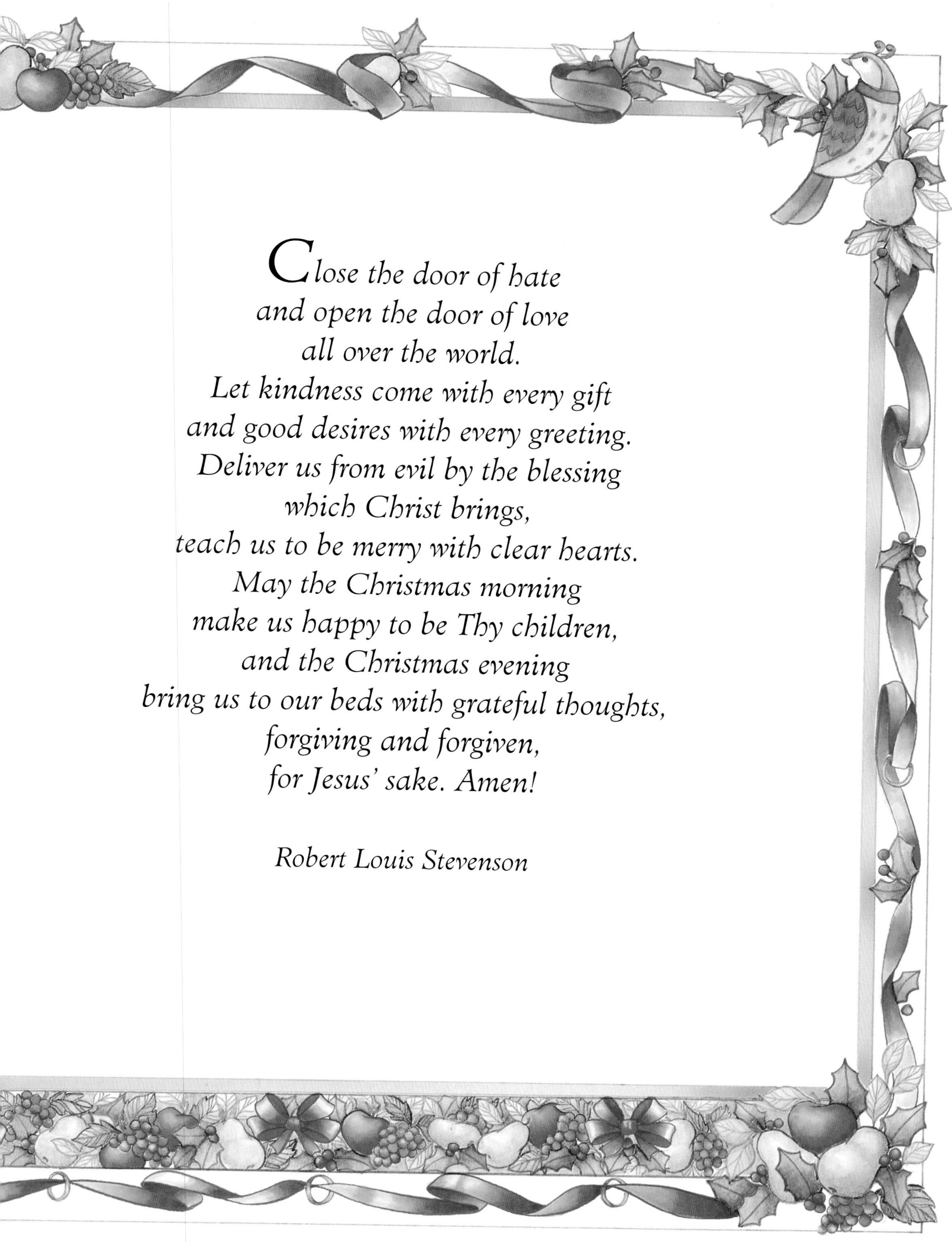

Close the door of hate
and open the door of love
all over the world.
Let kindness come with every gift
and good desires with every greeting.
Deliver us from evil by the blessing
which Christ brings,
teach us to be merry with clear hearts.
May the Christmas morning
make us happy to be Thy children,
and the Christmas evening
bring us to our beds with grateful thoughts,
forgiving and forgiven,
for Jesus' sake. Amen!

Robert Louis Stevenson

The Old Amaze

Grace Noll Crowell

These are the things I pray the years may leave
Untarnished and untouched by dust and blight:
The old amaze, the spell of Christmas Eve,
Its rapture and delight;

The breathless wonder that the stars awake;
The unfaltering belief that a star once led
Three kings a devious way—that it still can take
Men to Christ's manger bed.

And hurrying years, in passing let us keep
Some starry-eyed expectancy aglow:
The thing that children, waking from their sleep
On Christmas morning, know.

And, oh, some little flame of eagerness!
Years, leave it lighted as you pass, I pray:
A little inner flame to lift and bless
All hearts on Christmas Day.

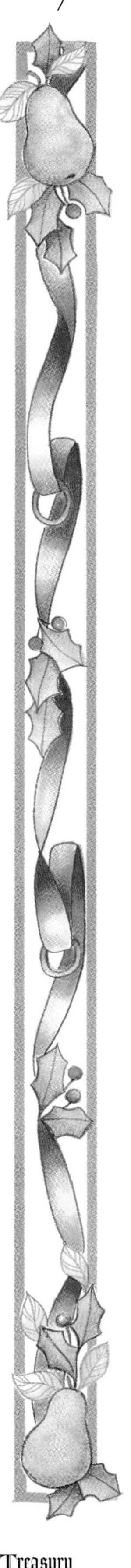

"And, lo, the star, which they saw in the east, went before them, till it came and stood over where the young child was."

Matthew 2:9

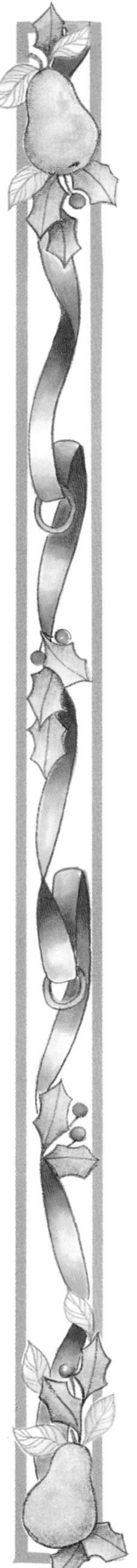

Christmas Was Coming

D. H. Lawrence

Gradually there gathered the feeling of expectation. Christmas was coming. In the shed, at nights, a secret candle was burning, a sound of veiled voices was heard. The boys were learning the old mystery play of St. George and Beelzebub. Twice a week, by lamplight, there was choir practice in the church, for the learning of old carols Brangwen wanted to hear. The girls went to these practices. Everywhere was a sense of mystery and rousedness. Everybody was preparing for something.

The time came near, the girls were decorating the church, with cold fingers binding holly and fir and yew about the pillars, till a new spirit was in the church, the stone broke out into dark, rich leaf, the arches put forth the aeuds, and cold flowers rose to blossom in the dim, mystic atmosphere. Ursula must weave mistletoe over the door, and over the screen, and hang a silver dove from a sprig of yew, till dusk came down, and the church was like a grove.

In the cow-shed the boys were blacking their faces for a dress-rehearsal; the turkey hung dead, with opened, speckled wings, in the dairy. The time was come to make pies, in readiness.

The expectation grew more tense. The star was risen into the sky, the songs, the carols were ready to hail it. The star was the sign in the sky. Earth too should give a sign. As evening drew on, hearts beat fast with anticipation, hands were full of ready gifts. There were the tremulously expectant words of the church service, the night was past and the morning was come, the gifts were given and received, joy and peace made a flapping of wings in each heart, there was a great burst of carols, the Peace of the World had dawned, strife had passed away, every hand was linked in hand, every heart was singing.

Christmas Sleigh Ride

Just before Christmas

Eugene Field

Father calls me William, sister calls me Will,
Mother calls me Willie, but the fellers call me Bill!
Mighty glad I ain't a girl—ruther be a boy,
Without them sashes, curls, an' things that's worn by Fauntleroy!
Love to chawnk green apples an' go swimmin' in the lake—
Hate to take the castor-ile they give for belly-ache!
'Most all the time, the whole year round, there ain't no flies on me,
But jest 'fore Christmas I'm as good as I kin be!

Got a yeller dog named Sport, sick him on the cat;
First thing she knows she doesn't know where she is at!
Got a clipper sled, an' when us kids goes out to slide,
'Long comes the grocery cart, an' we all hook a ride!
But sometimes when the grocery man is worried an' cross,
He reaches at us with his whip, an' larrups up his hoss,
An' then I laff an' holler, "Oh, ye never teched me!"
But jest 'fore Christmas I'm as good as I kin be!

Gran'ma says she hopes that when I git to be a man,
I'll be a missionarer like her oldest brother, Dan,
As was et up by the cannibals that lives in Ceylon's Isle,
Where every prospeck pleases, an' only man is vile!
But gran'ma she has never been to see a Wild West show,
Nor read the Life of Daniel Boone, or else I guess she'd know
That Buff'lo Bill an' cow-boys is good enough for me!
Excep' jest 'fore Christmas, when I'm good as I kin be!

And then old Sport he hangs around, so solemn-like an' still,
His eyes they seem a'sayin': "What's the matter, little Bill?"
The old cat sneaks down off her perch an' wonders what's become
Of them two enemies of hern that used to make things hum!
But I am so perlite an' 'tend so earnestly to biz,
That mother says to father: "How improved our Willie is!"
But father, havin' been a boy hisself, suspicions me
When, jest 'fore Christmas, I'm as good as I kin be!

For Christmas, with its lots an' lots of candies, cakes, an' toys,
Was made, they say, for proper kids, an' not for naughty boys;
So wash yer face an' bresh yer hair, an' mind year p's and q's
An' don't bust out yer pantaloons, and don't wear out yer shoes;
Say "Yessum" to the ladies, an' "Yessur" to the men,
An' when they's company, don't pass yer plate for pie again;
But, thinkin' of the things yer'd like to see upon that tree,
Jest 'fore Christmas be as good as yer kin be!

Baby's Ride
Unknown Nineteenth-Century Artist

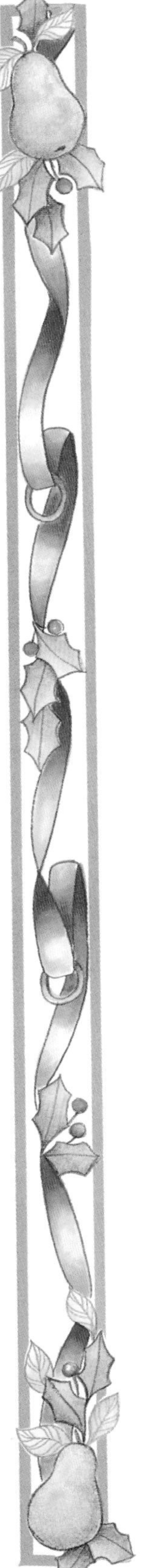

The Tree That Didn't Get Trimmed

Christopher Morley

If you walk through a grove of balsam trees you will notice that the young trees are silent; they are listening. But the old tall ones—especially the firs—are whispering. They are telling the story of The Tree That Didn't Get Trimmed. It sounds like a painful story, and the murmur of the old trees as they tell it is rather solemn; but it is an encouraging story for young saplings to hear. On warm autumn days when your trunk is tickled by ants and insects climbing, and the resin is hot and gummy in your knots, and the whole glade smells sweet, drowsy, and sad, and the hardwood trees are boasting of the gay colors they are beginning to show, many a young evergreen has been cheered by it.

All young fir trees, as you know by that story of Hans Andersen's—if you've forgotten it, why not read it again?—dream of being a Christmas Tree some day. They dream about it as young girls dream of being a bride, or young poets of having a volume of verse published. With the vision of that brightness and gaiety before them they patiently endure the sharp sting of the ax, the long hours pressed together on a freight car. But every December there are more trees cut down than are needed for Christmas. And that is the story that no one—not even Hans Andersen—has thought to put down.

The tree in this story should never have been cut. He wouldn't have been, but it was getting dark in the Vermont woods, and the man with the ax said to himself, "Just one more." Cutting young trees with a sharp, beautifully balanced ax is fascinating; you go on and on; there's a sort of cruel pleasure in it. The blade goes through the soft wood with one whistling stroke and the boughs sink down with a soft swish.

He was a fine, well-grown youngster, but too tall for his age; his branches were rather scraggly. If he'd been left there he would have been an unusually big tree some day; but now he was in the awkward age and didn't have the tapering shape and the thick, even foliage that people like on Christmas trees. Worse still, instead of running up to a straight, clean spire, his top was a bit lopsided, with a fork in it.

But he didn't know this as he stood with many others, leaning against the side wall of the greengrocer's shop. In those cold December days he was very happy thinking of the pleasures to come. He had heard of the delights of Christmas Eve: the stealthy setting up of the tree, the tinsel balls and colored toys and stars, the peppermint canes and birds with spun-glass tails. Even that old anxiety of Christmas trees—burning candles—did not worry him, for he had been told that nowadays people use strings of tiny electric bulbs which cannot set one on fire. So he looked forward to the festival with a confident heart.

"I shall be very grand," he said. "I hope there will be children to admire me. It must be a great moment when the children hang their stocking on you!" He even felt sorry for the first trees that were chosen and taken away. It would be best, he considered, not to be bought until Christmas Eve. Then, in the shining darkness someone would pick him out, put him carefully along the running board of a car, and away they would go. The tire chains would clack and jingle merrily on the snowy road. He imagined a big house with fire glowing on a hearth; the hushed rustle of wrapping paper and parcels being unpacked. Someone would say, "Oh, what a beautiful tree!" How erect and stiff he would brace himself in his iron tripod stand.

But day after day went by, one by one the other trees were taken, and he began to grow troubled. For everyone who looked at him seemed to have an unkind word. "Too tall," said one lady. "No, this one wouldn't do, the branches are too skimpy," said another. Some of his branches ached where the grocer had bent them upward to make his shape more attractive.

Across the street was a ten-cent store. Its bright windows were full of scarlet odds and ends; when the doors opened he could see people crowded along the aisles, cheerfully jostling one another with bumpy packages. A buzz of talk, a shuffle of feet, a constant ringing of cash drawers came noisily out of that doorway. He could see flashes of marvelous color, ornaments for luckier trees. Every evening, as the time drew nearer, the pavements were more thronged. The handsomer trees, not so tall as he but more bushy and shapely, were ranked in front of him; as they were taken away he could see the gaiety only too well. Then he was shown to a lady who wanted a tree very cheap. "You can have this one for a dollar," said the grocer. This was only one-third of what the grocer had asked for him at first, but even so the lady refused him and went across the street to buy a little artificial tree at the toy store. The man pushed him back carelessly, and he toppled over and fell alongside the wall. No one bothered to pick him up. He was almost glad, for now his pride would be spared.

Now it was Christmas Eve. It was a foggy evening with a drizzling rain; the alley alongside the store was thick with trampled slush. As he lay there among broken boxes and fallen scraps of holly, strange thoughts came to him. In the still northern forest already his wounded stump was buried in forgetful snow. He remembered the wintry sparkle of the woods, the big trees with crusts and clumps of silver on their broad boughs, the keen singing of the lonely wind. He remembered the strong, warm feeling of his roots reaching down into the safe earth. That is a good feeling; it means to a tree just what it means to you to stretch your toes down toward the bottom of a well-tucked bed. And he had given up all this to lie here, disdained and forgotten, in a littered alley. The splash of feet, the chime of bells, the cry of cars went past him. He trembled a little with self-pity and vexation. "No toys and stocking for me," he thought sadly, and shed some of his needles.

Late that night, after all the shopping was over, the grocer came out to clear away what was left. The boxes, the broken wreaths, the empty barrels, and our tree with one or two others that hadn't been sold, all were thrown through the side door into the cellar. The door was locked and he lay there in the dark. One of his branches, doubled under him in the fall, ached so he thought it must be broken. "So this is Christmas," he said to himself.

All that day it was very still in the cellar. There was an occasional creak as one of the bruised trees tried to stretch itself. Feet went along the pavement overhead, and there was a booming of church bells, but everything had a slow, disappointed sound. Christmas is always a little sad, after such busy preparations. The unwanted trees lay on the stone floor, watching the furnace light flick-

er on a hatchet that had been left there.

The day after Christmas a man came in who wanted some green boughs to decorate a cemetery. The grocer took the hatchet and seized the trees without ceremony. They were too disheartened to care. Chop, chop, chop, went the blade, and the sweet-smelling branches were carried away. The naked trunks were thrown into a corner.

And now our tree, what was left of him, had plenty of time to think. He no longer could feel anything, for trees feel with their branches, but they think with their trunks. What did he think about as he grew dry and stiff? He thought that it had been silly of him to imagine such a fine, gay career for himself, and he was sorry for other young trees, still growing in the fresh hilly country, who were enjoying the same fantastic dreams.

Now perhaps you don't know what happens to the trunks of leftover Christmas trees. You could never guess. Farmers come in from the suburbs and buy them at five cents each for bean poles and grape arbors. So perhaps (here begins the encouraging part of this story) they are really happier, in the end, than the trees that get trimmed for Santa Claus. They go back into the fresh moist earth of spring, and when the sun grows hot the quick tendrils of the vines climb up them and presently they are decorated with the red blossoms of the bean or the little blue globes of the grape, just as pretty as any Christmas trinkets.

So one day the naked, dusty fir poles were taken out of the cellar, and thrown into a truck with many others, and made a rattling journey out into the land. The farmer unloaded them in his yard and was stacking them up by the barn when his wife came out to watch him.

"There!" she said. "That's just what I want, a nice long pole with a fork in it. Jim, put that one over there to hold up the clothesline." It was the first time that anyone had praised our tree, and his dried-up heart swelled with a tingle of forgotten sap. They put him near one end of the clothesline, with his stump close to a flower bed. The fork that had been despised for a Christmas star was just the thing to hold up a clothesline. It was, and soon the farmer's wife began bringing out wet garments to swing and freshen in the clean bright air. And the very first thing that hung near the top of the Christmas pole was a cluster of children's stockings.

That isn't quite the end of the story, as the old fir trees whisper it in the breeze. The Tree That Didn't Get Trimmed was so cheerful watching the stocking, and other gay little clothes that plumped out in the wind just as though waiting to be spanked, that he didn't notice what was going on—or going up—below him. A vine had caught hold of his trunk and was steadily twisting upward. And one morning, when the farmer's wife came out intending to shift him, she stopped and exclaimed. "Why, I mustn't move this pole," she said. "The morning glory has run right up it." So it had, and our bare pole was blue and crimson with color.

Something nice, the old firs believe, always happens to the trees that don't get trimmed. They even believe that someday one of the Christmas-tree bean poles will be the starting point for another Magic Beanstalk, as in the fairy tale of the boy who climbed up the bean tree and killed the giant. When that happens, fairy tales will begin all over again.

Heavy snow on trees
Cornwall, Connecticut

O Little Town of Bethlehem
Phillips Brooks
Lewis H. Redner
O lit-tle town of Beth-le-hem, How still we see thee lie! A-
bove thy deep and dream-less sleep The si-lent stars go by; Yet
in thy dark streets shin-eth The ev-er-last-ing Light; The
hopes and fears of all the years Are met in thee to-night.

For Christ is born of Mary;
And gather'd all above,
While mortals sleep, the angels keep
Their watch of wond'ring love.
O morning stars together
Proclaim Thy holy birth
And praises sing to God the King
And peace to men on earth.

How silently, how silently,
The wondrous gift is given!
So God imparts to human hearts
The blessings of his heaven.
No ear may hear his coming,
But in this world of sin,
Where meek souls will receive him still
The dear Christ enters in.

O holy Child of Bethlehem,
Descend to us we pray;
Cast out our sin and enter in;
Be born to us today.
We hear the Christmas angels,
The great glad tidings tell;
O come to us, abide with us,
Our Lord Emmanuel.

Santa Is Coming

Edgar A. Guest

It's "be a good boy, Willie,"
And it's "run away and play,
For Santa Claus is coming
With his reindeer and his sleigh."
It's "mind what mother tells you."
And it's "put-away your toys,
For Santa Claus is coming
To the good girls and the boys."
Ho, Santa Claus is coming,
there is Christmas in the air,
And little girls and little boys are good
now everywhere

World-wide the little fellows
Now are sweetly saying "please,"
And "thank you," and "excuse me,"
And those little pleasantries
That good children are supposed to
When there's company to hear;
And it's just as plain as can be that
old Santa's on his way
For there are no little children that are
really bad today.

And when evening shadows lengthen,
Every little curly head
Now is ready, aye, and willing
To be tucked away in bed;
Not one begs to stay up longer,
Not one even sheds a tear;
Ho, the goodness of the children
Is a sign that Santa's near.
It's wonderful the goodness of the little
tots today,
When they know that good old Santa has
begun to pack his sleigh.

Here Comes the Christmas Tree
Unknown Nineteenth- or Twentieth- Century Artist

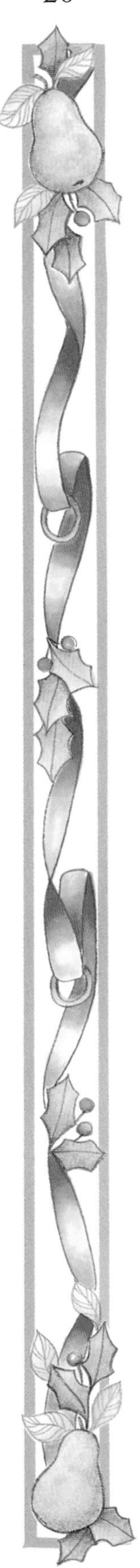

Going Home for Christmas

Edgar A. Guest

He little knew the sorrow that was in his vacant chair,
He never guessed they'd miss him, or he'd surely have been there,
He couldn't see his mother or the lump that filled her throat,
Or the tears that started falling as she read his hasty note;
And he couldn't see his father, sitting sorrowful and dumb,
Or he never would have written that he thought he couldn't come.

He couldn't see the fading of the cheeks that once were pink,
And the silver in the tresses, and he didn't stop to think
How the years are passing swiftly, and next Christmas it might be
There would be no home to visit and no mother dear to see.
He didn't think about it—I'll not say he didn't care,
He was heedless and forgetful or he'd surely have been there.

Are you going home for Christmas? Have you written you'll be there?
Going home to kiss the mother and to show her that you care?
Going home to greet the father in a way to make him glad?
If you're not I hope there'll never come a time you'll wish you had.
Just sit down and write a letter—it will make their heart strings hum
With a tune of perfect gladness—if you'll tell them that you'll come.

Oh, how joyfully, Oh, how merrily,
Christmas comes with its grace divine!
Grace again is beaming,
Christ the world redeeming:
Hail, ye Christians,
Hail the joyous Christmastime!

J. Falk

Village and Church through Sugar Maples
East Orange, Vermont

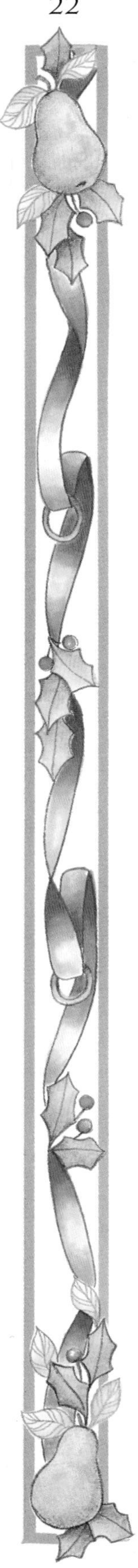

Meditation on Christmas Eve

Angelo Guiseppe Roncalli

Night has fallen; the clear, bright stars are sparkling in the cold air; noisy, strident voices rise to my car from the city, voices of the revelers of this world who celebrate with merrymaking the poverty of their Saviour. Around me in their rooms my companions are asleep, and I am still wakeful, thinking of the mystery of Bethlehem.

Come, come, Jesus, I await you.

Mary and Joseph, knowing the hour is near, are turned away by the townsfolk and go out into the fields to look for a shelter. I am a poor shepherd; I have only a wretched stable, a small manger, some wisps of straw. I offer all these to you, be pleased to come into my poor hovel. I offer you my heart; my soul is poor and bare of virtues, the straws of so many imperfections will prick you and make you weep—but oh, my lord, what can you expect? This little is all I have. I am touched by your poverty, I am moved to tears, but I have nothing better to offer you, Jesus; honour my soul with your presence, adorn it with your graces. Burn this straw and change it into a soft couch for your most holy body.

Jesus, I am here waiting for your coming. Wicked men have driven you out, and the wind is like ice. I am a poor man, but I will warm you as well as I can. At least be pleased that I wish to welcome you warmly, to love you and sacrifice myself for you.

The Nativity
Carl Van Leo, 1705-1765

Christmas Is for Joy

*Somehow, not only
for Christmas
But all the year through,
The joy that you give
to others
is the joy that comes
back to you;
and the more you spend in blessing
the poor and lonely
and sad,
the more of your heart's
possessing
returns to make you glad.*

John Greenleaf Whittier

A. CHEVALLIER TAYLER

Happy, Happy Christmas

Charles Dickens

Christmas time! That man must be a misanthrope indeed, in whose breast something like a jovial feeling is not roused—in whose mind some pleasant associations are not awakened—by the recurrence of Christmas. There are people who will tell you that Christmas is not to them what it used to be; that each succeeding Christmas has found some cherished hope, or happy prospect, of the year before, dimmed or passed away; that the present only serves to remind them of reduced circumstances and straitened incomes—of the feasts they once bestowed on hollow friends, and of the cold looks that meet them now, in adversity and misfortune. Never heed such dismal reminiscences. There are few men who have lived long enough in the world, who cannot call up such thoughts any day in the year. Then do not select the merriest of the three hundred and sixty-five for your doleful recollections, but draw your chair nearer the blazing fire—fill the glass and send round the song—and if your room be smaller than it was a dozen years ago, or if your glass be filled with reeking punch, instead of sparkling wine, put a good face on the matter, and empty it off-hand, and fill another, and troll off the old ditty you used to sing, and thank God it's no worse. . . .

Who can be insensible to the outpourings of good feeling, and the honest interchange of affectionate attachment which abound at this season of the year. A Christmas family-party! We know nothing in nature more delightful! There seems a magic in the very name of Christmas. Petty jealousies and discords are forgotten; social feelings are awakened, in bosoms to which they have long been strangers; father and son, or brother and sister, who have met and passed with averted gaze, or a look of cold recognition, for months before, proffer and return the cordial embrace, and bury their past animosities in their present happiness. Kindly hearts that have yearned towards each other but have been withheld by false notions of pride and self-dignity, are again reunited, and all is kindness and benevolence! Would that Christmas lasted the whole year through (as it ought) and that the prejudices and passions which deform our better nature were never called into action among those to whom they should ever be strangers.

The Christmas Tree
Albert Chevallier Tayler, 1862-1925

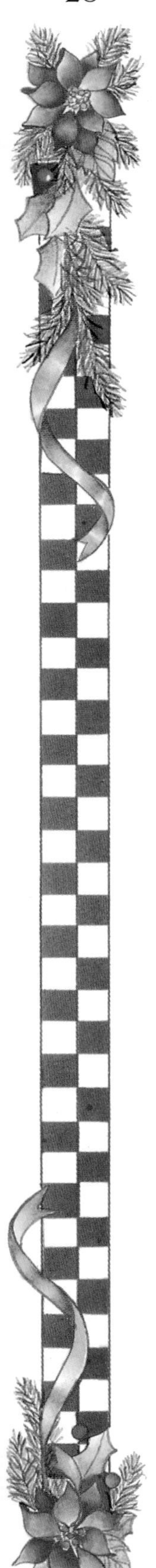

My Christmas Miracle

Taylor Caldwell

For many of us, one Christmas stands out from all the others, the one when the meaning of the day shone clearest. Although I did not guess it, my own "truest" Christmas began on a rainy spring day in the bleakest year of my life. Recently divorced, I was in my twenties, had no job, and was on my way downtown to go the rounds of the employment offices. I had no umbrella, for my old one had fallen apart, and I could not afford another one. I sat down in the streetcar; and there against the seat was a beautiful silk umbrella with a silver handle inlaid with gold and flecks of bright enamel. I had never seen anything so lovely.

I examined the handle and saw a name engraved among the golden scrolls. The usual procedure would have been to turn in the umbrella to the conductor; but on impulse I decided to take it with me and find the owner myself. I got off the streetcar in a downpour and thankfully opened the umbrella to protect myself. Then I searched a telephone book for the name on the umbrella and found it. I called and a lady answered.

Yes, she said in surprise, that was her umbrella, which her parents, now dead, had given her for a birthday present. But, she added, it had been stolen from her locker at school (she was a teacher) more than a year before. She was so excited that I forgot I was looking for a job and went directly to her small house. She took the umbrella, and her eyes filled with tears.

The teacher wanted to give me a reward, but—though twenty dollars was all I had in the world—her happiness at retrieving this special possession was such that to have accepted money would have spoiled something. We talked for a while, and I must have given her my address. I don't remember.

The next six months were wretched. I was able to obtain only temporary employment here and there, for a small salary, though this was what they now call the Roaring Twenties. But I put aside twenty-five or fifty cents when I could afford it for my little girl's Christmas presents. (It took me six months to save eight dollars.) My last job ended the day before Christmas, my thirty dollar rent was soon due, and I had fifteen dollars to my name—which Peggy and I would need for food. She was home from her convent boarding school and was excitedly looking forward to her gifts the next day, which I had already purchased. I had bought her a small tree, and we were going to decorate it that night.

The stormy air was full of the sound of Christmas merriment as I walked from the streetcar to my small apartment. Bells rang and children shouted in the bitter dusk of the evening, and windows were lighted and everyone was running and laughing. But there would be no Christmas for me, I knew, no gifts, no remembrance whatsoever. As I struggled through the snowdrifts, I just about reached the lowest point in my life. Unless a miracle happened, I would be homeless in January, foodless, jobless. I had prayed steadily for weeks, and there had been no answer but this

Antique Christmas Greeting Card

A merry Christmas
SER.12

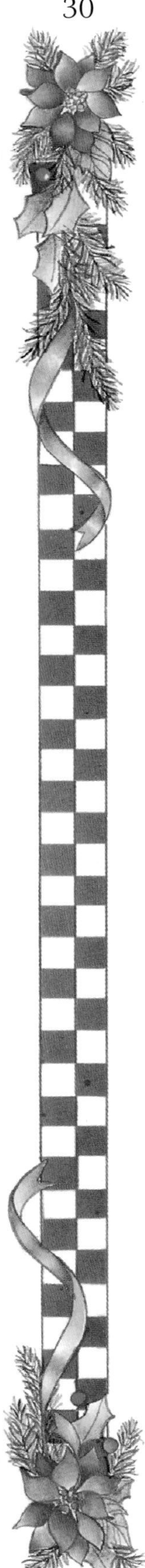

coldness and darkness, this harsh air, this abandonment. God and men had completely forgotten me. I felt old as death, and as lonely. What was to become of us?

I looked in my mailbox. There were only bills in it, a sheaf of them, and two white envelopes which I was sure contained more bills. I went up three dusty flights of stairs, and I cried, shivering in my thin coat. But I made myself smile so I could greet my little daughter with a pretense of happiness. She opened the door for me and threw herself in my arms, screaming joyously and demanding that we decorate the tree immediately.

Peggy was not yet six years old, and had been alone all day while I worked. She had proudly set our kitchen table for our evening meal and put pans out and the three cans of food which would be our dinner. For some reason, when I looked at those pans and cans, I felt brokenhearted. We would have only hamburgers for our Christmas dinner tomorrow, and gelatin. I stood in the cold little kitchen, and misery overwhelmed me. For the first time in my life, I doubted the existence of God and his mercy, and the coldness in my heart was colder than ice.

The doorbell rang and Peggy ran fleetly to answer it, calling that it must be Santa Claus. Then I heard a man talking heartily to her and went to the door. He was a delivery man, and his arms were full of parcels, and he was laughing at my child's frenzied joy and her dancing. "This is a mistake," I said, but he read the name on the parcels and they were for me. When he had gone I could only stare at the boxes. Peggy and I sat on the floor and opened them. A huge doll, three times the size of the one I had bought for her. Gloves. Candy. A beautiful leather purse. Incredible! I looked for the name of the sender. It was the teacher, the address simply "California," where she had moved.

Our dinner that night was the most delicious I had ever eaten, I could only pray to myself, "Thank you, Father." I forgot I had no money for the rent and only fifteen dollars in my purse and no job. My child and I ate and laughed together in happiness. Then we decorated the little tree and marveled at it. I put Peggy to bed and set up her gifts around the tree, and a sweet peace flooded me like a benediction. I had some hope again. I could even examine the sheaf of bills without cringing. Then I opened the two white envelopes. One contained a check for thirty dollars from a company I had worked for briefly in the summer. It was, said a note, my "Christmas bonus:" My Rent!

The other envelope was an offer of a permanent position with the government—to begin two days after Christmas. I sat with the letter in my hand and the check on the table before me, and I think that was the most joyful moment of my life up to that time.

The church bells began to ring. I hurriedly looked at my child, who was sleeping blissfully, and ran down to the street. Everywhere people were walking to church to celebrate the birth of the Savior. People smiled at me and I smiled back. The storm had stopped, the sky was pure and glittering with stars.

"The Lord is born!" sang the bells to the crystal night and the laughing darkness. Someone began to sing, "Come, all ye faithful!" I joined in and sang with the strangers all about me.

I am not alone at all, I thought. I was never alone at all.

And that, of course, is the message of Christmas. We are never alone. Not when the night is darkest, the wind coldest, the world seemingly most indifferent. For this is still the time God chooses.

Steady Now!
Unknown Nineteenth-Century Artist

Nick

Joy to the World

Isaac Watts

Joy to the world!
The Lord has come:
Let earth receive her King;
Let every heart prepare Him room,
And heaven and nature sing,
And heaven and nature sing,
And heaven, and heaven, and nature sing.

Joy to the world!
The Saviour reigns.
Let men their songs employ,
While fields and floods,
Rocks, hills, aand plains,
Repeat the sounding joy,
Repeat the sounding joy,
Repeat, repeat the sounding joy.

No more let sin and sorrow grow,
Nor thorns infest the ground;
He comes to make His blessings flow;
Far as the curse is found,
Far as the curse is found,
Far as, far as the curse is found.

He rules the world with truth and grace,
And makes the nations prove
The glories of His righteousness
And wonders of His love,
And wonders of His love,
And wonders, wonders of His love.

Christmas with the Little Women

Louisa May Alcott

"Christmas won't be Christmas without any presents," grumbled Jo, lying on the rug.

"It's so dreadful to be poor!" sighed Meg, looking down at her old dress.

"We've got Father and Mother and each other," said Beth contentedly from her corner.

The four young faces on which the firelight shone brightened at the cheerful words.

"The reason Mother proposed not having any presents this Christmas was because it is going to be a hard winter for everyone," Meg said. "She thinks we ought not to spend money for pleasure. We can't do much, but we can make our little sacrifices, and ought to do it gladly. But I am afraid I don't." And Meg shook her head, as she thought regretfully of all the pretty things she wanted.

"Mother didn't say anything about our money, and she won't wish us to give up everything. Let's each buy what we want and have a little fun. I'm sure we work hard enough to earn it," cried Jo.

As young readers like to know "how people look," we will take this moment to give them a little sketch of the four sisters, who sat knitting away in the twilight, while the December snow fell quietly without, and the fire crackled cheerfully within.

Meg, the oldest of the four, was sixteen, and very pretty, with large eyes, plenty of soft, brown hair, a sweet mouth, and white hands, of which she was rather vain.

Fifteen-year-old Jo was very tall and thin and reminded one of a colt, for she never seemed to know what to do with her long limbs. She had a decided mouth, a comical nose, and sharp, gray eyes, which appeared to see everything, and were by turns fierce, funny, or thoughtful. Her long, thick hair was her one beauty, but it was usually bundled into a net, to be out of her way. Jo had round shoulders, big hands and feet, a flyaway look to her clothes, and the uncomfortable appearance of a girl who was rapidly shooting up into a woman.

Elizabeth—or Beth, as everyone called her—was a rosy, smooth-haired, bright-eyed girl of thirteen, with a shy manner, a timid voice, and a peaceful expression which was seldom disturbed. Her father called her

Gathering Round the Christmas Tre
Unknown Nineteenth-Century Arti

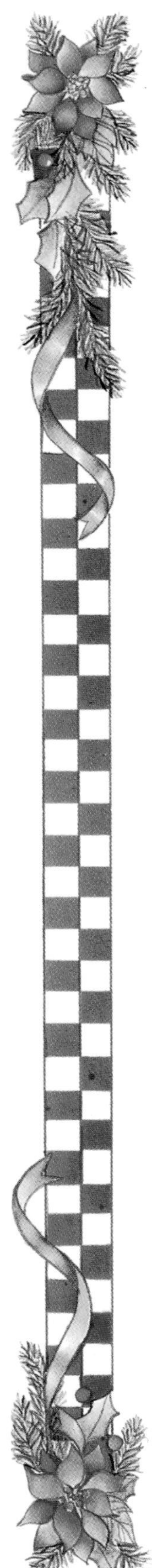

"Little Tranquility," and the name suited her excellently.

Amy, though the youngest, was a most important person—in her opinion at least. A regular snow maiden, with blue eyes, and yellow hair curling on her shoulders, pale and slender, and always carrying herself like a young lady mindful of her manners.

The clock struck six and, having swept up the hearth, Beth put a pair of slippers down to warm. Somehow the sight of the old shoes had a good effect upon the girls, for Mother was coming, and everyone brightened to welcome her home. Meg stopped lecturing and lighted the lamp, Amy got out of the easy chair without being asked, and Jo forgot how tired she was as she sat up to hold the slippers nearer to the blaze.

"They are quite worn out. Marmee must have a new pair."

"I'll tell you what we'll do," said Beth, "let's each get something for Marmee for Christmas, and not get anything for ourselves."

"That's like you, dear! What will we get?" exclaimed Jo.

Everyone thought soberly for a minute, then Meg announced, "I shall give her a nice pair of gloves."

"Army shoes, the very best to be had," cried Jo.

"Some handkerchiefs, all hemmed," said Beth.

"I'll get a little bottle of cologne. She likes it, and it won't cost much, so I'll have some left to buy my pencils," added Amy.

"Let Marmee think we are getting things for ourselves, and then surprise her. We must go shopping tomorrow afternoon, Meg," said Jo, marching up and down, with her hands behind her back and her nose in the air.

"Glad to find you so merry, my girls," said a cheery voice at the door, and the girls turned to welcome a tall, motherly lady with a "can-I-help-you" look about her which was truly delightful. She was not elegantly dressed, but the girls thought the gray cloak and unfashionable bonnet covered the most splendid mother in the world.

"Well, dearies, how have you got on today? Has anyone called, Beth? How is your cold, Meg? Jo, you look tired to death. Come and kiss me, baby."

While making these maternal inquiries Mrs. March got her wet things off, her warm slippers on, and sitting down in the easy chair, drew Amy to her lap, preparing to enjoy the happiest hour of her busy day.

At nine they stopped work, and sang, as usual, before they went to bed. No one but Beth could get much music out of the old piano, but she had a way of softly touching the yellow keys and making a pleasant accompaniment to the simple songs they sang.

Jo was the first to wake in the gray dawn of Christmas morning. No stockings hung at the fireplace, and for a moment she felt disappointed. Then she slipped her hand under her pillow and drew out a crimson-covered Bible.

She woke Meg with a "Merry Christmas," and bade her see what was under pillow. A green-covered Bible appeared, with a few words written by their mother, which made their one present very precious in their eyes. Presently Beth and Amy woke to rummage and find their little books also—one dove-colored, the other blue—and all sat looking at and talking about their little books, while the east grew rosy with the coming day.

"Girls," said Meg seriously, looking from the tumbled head beside her to the two little nightcapped ones in the room beyond, "Mother wants us to read and love and mind these books, and we must begin at once. You can do as you please, but I shall keep my book on the table here and read a little every morning as soon as I wake, for I know it will do me good and help me through the day."

"How good Meg is! Come, Amy, let's do as they do. I'll help you with the hard words, and they'll explain things if we don't understand," whispered Beth, very much impressed by the pretty books and her sisters' example.

The rooms were very still while the pages were softly turned, and the winter sunshine crept in to touch the bright heads and serious faces with a Christmas greeting.

"But peaceful was the night
Wherein the Prince of Light
His reign of peace
upon the earth began."
John Milton

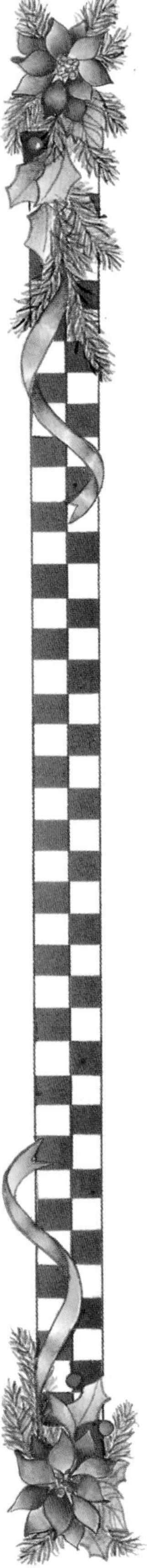

A Christmas Tree

Charles Dickens

I have been looking on, this evening, at a merry company of children assembled round that pretty German toy, a Christmas Tree. The tree was planted in the middle of a great round table, and towered high above their heads. It was brilliantly lighted by a multitude of little tapers; and everywhere sparkled and glittered with bright objects. There were rosy-cheeked dolls, hiding behind the green leaves; and there were real watches (with movable hands, at least, and an endless capacity of being wound up) dangling from innumerable twigs; there were French-polished tables, chairs, bedsteads, wardrobes, eight-day clocks, and various other articles of domestic furniture (wonderfully made, in tin, at Wolverhampton) perched among the boughs, as if in preparation for some fairy housekeeping; there were jolly, broad-faced little men, much more agreeable in appearance than many real men—and no wonder, for their heads took off, and showed them to be full of sugar-plums; there were fiddles and drums; there were tambourines, books, work-boxes, paintboxes, sweetmeat boxes, peep-show boxes, and all kinds of boxes; there were trinkets for the elder girls, far brighter than any grown-up gold and jewels; there were baskets and pincushions in all devices; there were guns, swords, and banners; there were witches standing in enchanted rings of pasteboard, to tell fortunes; there were teetotums, humming-tops, needle-cases, pen-wipers, smelling-bottles, conversation-cards, bouquet-holders; real fruit, made artificially dazzling with gold leaf; imitation apples, pears, and walnuts, crammed with surprises; in short, as a pretty child, before me, delightedly whispered to another pretty child, her bosom friend, "There was everything, and more."

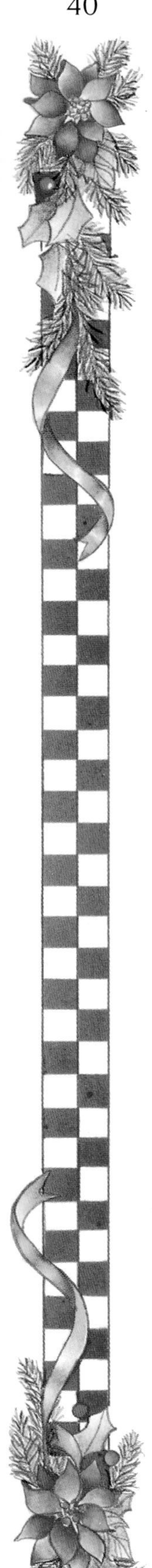

A Christmas Carol

Charles Dickens

Old Scrooge was a tight-fisted man, he was! Why, old Jacob Marley had been dead for seven years, yet Scrooge had not even had Marley's name painted out over the door to the counting house.

Now once upon a time on a cold and groggy Christmas Eve, Scrooge sat counting his money in his counting house. The door to his office was open so he could keep an eye on his clerk, Bob Cratchit. Poor Bob was wrapped in a long woolen muffler because Scrooge was too stingy to allow him a fire.

With a sudden gust of wind, the door flew open as Scrooge's nephew stepped in to wish his uncle a "Merry Christmas." The only reply from Scrooge was a harsh "Bah humbug!"

Moments after his nephew's departure, the door was pushed open again, and two gentlemen entered.

"Good day, kind sir," said one. "We are raising funds for the poor this Christmas season. What shall I put you down for?"

"Nothing!" replied Scrooge. "It is no concern of mine if these folks are poor."

The two men shook their heads at his angry words and turned to leave.

Scrooge turned to look at his clerk. "I suppose you want all day tomorrow off. You may have it," he said grudgingly, "but you had better be in early the next day."

And with that, Scrooge stomped out the door and headed home.

As Scrooge began to turn the key in his door, he noticed something strange about the big brass knocker on the door. From the center of it glowed a ghostly face, with spectacles upon its forehead.

Christmas Comes But Once a Year!
Unknown Artist for Pears' Soap Print, 1896

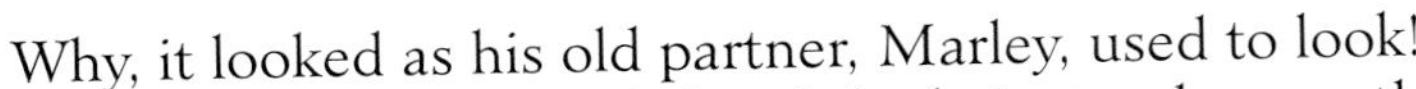
Why, it looked as his old partner, Marley, used to look!

Scrooge's spine tingled and the hair stood up on the back of his neck. As he stared at the ghostly face, it became a knocker again. He dashed into the house and up into his room where he locked the door twice.

As Scrooge sat alone sipping a small bowl of gruel, his mind returned to the knocker. "Humbug!" he said to himself.

No sooner had he said this than strange noises began to sound. And right through the twice-locked door, a ghost appeared, a ghost dressed in Marley's coat and boots, but also wrapped in chains made of keys, cashboxes, and bankbooks!

"Who are you?" Scrooge whispered. "What do you want?"

"Much," said the ghost of Marley. "I lived a wasted and selfish life—caring only about money—and now I must wander like this forever, weighed down by these chains. But you, Ebenezer, have yet a chance to escape my fate.

"You will be haunted," the ghost continued, "by three spirits. Expect the first tomorrow when the clock strikes one. You will see me no more, but remember what I have said."

And with that, the ghost of Jacob Marley slipped out the window into the foggy night air. And Scrooge turned and went straight to bed.

When Scrooge awoke, he heard the clock strike one in the stillness of the night. Suddenly a strange figure stood beside his bed. It had long white hair, but a smooth fair face without a wrinkle. And from its head, a beam of light glowed.

Scrooge clutched his blankets to his chin and asked, "Are you the Spirit whose coming was foretold to me?"

"Yes," it said. "I am the Spirit of Christmas Past. Rise and walk with me."

They were instantly transported to the office where Scrooge had worked as a young man.

"Why, it's Old Fezziwig!" exclaimed Scrooge.

As he watched, his old boss slapped a younger Scrooge on the back and said, "No more work tonight, it's Christmas Eve. Let's clear the floor and set up for a party."

Watching this delightful scene, Scrooge thought back to yet another Christmas past. He sat beside a young girl whose eyes were filled with tears.

"I cannot marry you, Ebenezer," she said softly, "for you love another more than me."

"There is no one else," argued Scrooge.

"Not someone, but something," she said. "You love your money more than me." A single tear ran down her cheek, then she turned and left.

"Spirit," Scrooge cried. "Show me no more. Take me home."

"Come then," the Spirit answered. "My time is short. We must return."

Immediately Scrooge was back in his own room, on his bed in a heavy sleep.

Awaking in the middle of a snore, Scrooge again heard the clock strike one. Looking around, he saw his room; and yet something was strange. The room was not as he remembered.

The walls were hung with holly, and a roaring fire filled the room with light. And heaped on the floor was a steaming, fragrant feast.

Seated amidst this feast was an enormous, laughing giant. "Come in," he boomed. "I am the Spirit of Christmas Present."

He reached his hand toward Scrooge and commanded, "Touch my robe."

Instantly they were transported through the snowy streets to the house of poor Bob Cratchit. It was a simple house, yet filled with life and love.

Tiny Tim, a small, pale child who carried a crutch, sat close to his father. As the Christmas meal drew to a close, Bob raised his cup and said, "A Merry Christmas to us all. God bless us."

"God bless us every one!" cried Tiny Tim.

Bob held his son's small hand in his own, for he loved the child and feared Tiny Tim would not live to see another Christmas.

"Spirit," said Scrooge. "Tell me if Tiny Tim will live."

"I see an empty chair," replied the Spirit. "If these shadows remain unchanged by the future, then the child will die."

When the clock struck again, the Spirit disappeared.

Frightened, Scrooge peered into the darkness around him. He saw a dark and frightening shape moving toward him. Beneath the shadowy hood of the Spirit's robe, two ghostly eyes pierced him with an icy stare.

"Are you the Ghost of Christmas Yet to Come?" he asked.

The Spirit nodded slightly and began to move ahead. Scrooge followed in its shadow. They came to the home of Bob Cratchit, where they noticed Tiny Tim's empty chair in a corner.

"Oh, Father," cried one of the girls. "What shall we do without our Tiny Tim?"

"We shall not forget him, dear," Bob answered, wiping a tear from his eye. We shall always remember how kind and patient he was."

Then the Spirit carried Scrooge away to an old weed-choked churchyard. In the deeply carved granite of one of the stones, his name could be read—EBENEZER SCROOGE.

He shrieked, "Oh, hear me, Spirit! Tell me I have hope of changing what you have shown me. I will honor Christmas in my heart and try to keep it all year. Help me change the future as I saw it here!"

He caught the Spirit's hand; but as he did so, it changed into a bedpost—his bedpost.

"I will live in the past, the present, and the future," Scrooge cried joyfully as he climbed out of bed. "Oh, thank you, Jacob Marley. Thank you most sincerely!"

And Ebenezer Scrooge was better than his word. He did it all and even more; and to Tiny Tim, who did not die, he was a second father. He became as good a friend, master, and man as anyone ever knew. From that day on, it was always said that Ebenezer Scrooge knew how to keep Christmas well.

May that be said of each of us. And so, as Tiny Tim observed: God bless us every one!

Christmas Is for Love

Have you any old grudges
you would like to pay,
Any wrongs laid up
from a bygone day?
Gather them now
and lay them away
When Christmas comes.
Hard thoughts are heavy
to carry, my friend,
And life is short
from beginning to end;
Be kind to yourself,
leave nothing to mend
When Christmas comes.

William Lytle

Keeping Christmas

Henry Van Dyke

It is a good thing to observe Christmas day. The mere marking of times and seasons, when men agree to stop work and make merry together, is a wise and wholesome custom. It helps one to feel the supremacy of the common life over the individual life. It reminds a man to set his own little watch, now and then, by the great clock of humanity which runs on sun time.

But there is a better thing than the observance of Christmas day, and that is, keeping Christmas.

Are you willing to forget what you have done for other people, and to remember what other people have done for you; to ignore what the world owes you, and to think what you owe the world; to put your rights in the background, and your duties in the middle distance, and your chances to do a little more than your duty in the foreground; to see that your fellow-men are just as real as you are, and try to look behind their faces to their hearts, hungry for joy; to own that probably the only good reason for your existence is not what you are going to get out of life, but what you are going to give to life; to close your book of complaints against the management of the universe, and look around you for a place where you can sow a few seeds of happiness—are you willing to do these things even for a day? Then you can keep Christmas.

Are you willing to stoop down and consider the needs and the desires of little children; to remember the weakness and loneliness of people who are growing old; to stop asking how much your friends love you, and ask yourself whether you love them enough; to bear in mind the things that other people have to bear in their hearts; to try to understand that those who live in the same house with you really want, without waiting for them to tell you; to trim your lamp so that it will give more light and less smoke, and to carry it in front so that your shadow will fall behind you; to make a grave for your ugly thoughts and a garden for your kindly feelings, with the gate open—are you willing to do these things even for a day? Then you can keep Christmas.

Are you willing to believe that love is the strongest thing in the world—stronger than hate, stronger than evil, stronger than death—and that the blessed life which began in Bethlehem nineteen hundred years ago is the image and brightness of the Eternal Love? Then you can keep Christmas.

And if you keep it for a day, why not always?

But you can never keep it alone.

Christmas Bounty

A Christmas Gift

T.F. Powys

It is a harmless wish to like a little notice to be taken of one's name, and a number of people, besides Mr. Balliboy, the Dodder carrier, like attention to be paid to their names when they are written down. Children will write their names upon a fair stretch of yellow sand, young men will carve their names upon an old oak in the forest, and even the most simple peasant will like to see his name printed in a newspaper.

For most of his life Mr. Balliboy was satisfied with having his name written upon the side of his van, and he was always pleased and interested when anyone paused in the street to read his name.

But Mr. Balliboy's pride in his name made him do more than one foolish thing.

Once he cut "Mr. Balliboy, Carrier," with his market knife upon one of the doors of Mr. Told's old barn, and again upon the right-hand post of the village pound. But, on his going to see how the names looked the next Sunday,—and perhaps hoping that a stranger might be found regarding them,—he discovered, to his sorrow, that the rude village boys had changed the first letters of his name into an unpleasant and ill-sounding word.

Mr. Balliboy was a lonely man, and a bachelor—for no young woman would ever look at his name twice and none had ever wished to have his name written beside hers in a church register.

One Christmas Mr. Balliboy journeyed, as was his wont, to Weyminster. His van was full of country women, each one of whom thought herself to be of the highest quality, for each had put on the finest airs with her market clothes and, so dressed, could talk in a superior manner.

Mr. Balliboy had certainly one reason for happiness—other than the ordinary joyfulness of the merry season—which was that his rival, John Hawkins, had passed by with his van empty of customers,—yet Mr. Balliboy was sad. His sadness came, strangely enough, only because he wished, for the first time in his life, to give a Christmas present.

It might have been only to give himself pleasure that he wished to do this. For whatever the present was that he should buy, he determined that a label should be tied on it, with his name clearly upon it—"From Mr. Balliboy."

What the present would be, and to whom it should be given, Mr. Balliboy did not know. He decided to buy something that he fancied, and then allow destiny to decide to whom the gift should go.

When Mr. Balliboy reached the town he walked about the streets in order to see what could be bought for money. Many a shop window did he look into and many a time did he stand and scratch his head, wondering what he should buy.

There was one oddity that he fancied in a toyshop,—a demon holding a fork in his hand, upon which he was raising a naked young woman. Mr. Balliboy thought the demon might do, but over the young woman he shook his head.

Mr. Balliboy moved to another window. Here at once, he saw what pleased him—a little cross, made of cardboard and covered with tinsel, that shone and glistened before Mr. Balliboy's admiring eyes.

Mr. Balliboy purchased the cross for a shilling and attached a label to it, with his name written large. . . .

Sometimes a change comes over a scene, now so happy and gay but in one moment altered into a frown. As soon as Mr. Balliboy had buttoned the cross into his pocket the streets of Weyminster showed this changed look. The shoppers' merriment and joyful surprise at what they saw in the windows gave place to a sad and tired look. The great church that so many hurried by in order to reach their favorite tavern, appeared more dark and somber than a winter's day should ever have made it.

Even the warm drinks served out by black-haired Mabel at the "Rod and Lion" could not make the drinkers forget that care and trouble could cut a Christmas cake and sing a Christmas carol as well as they.

The general gloom of the town touched Mr. Balliboy, and had he not had the present hid in his coat, he might have entered an Inn, in order to drown the troubled feelings that moved about him, in a deep mug.

But, having bought the Christmas present, he had now the amusement of seeking the right person to give it to. And so, instead of walking along the street with downcast eyes, he walked along smiling.

While he was yet some way off his van, he he could see that a figure was standing beside it, who seemed to be reading his name. And, whoever this was, Mr. Balliboy determined as he walked, that it should be the one to receive his Christmas gift.

As he drew near he saw that the figure was that of a young woman—wrapped in a thin cloak—who showed by her wan look and by her shape that she expected soon to be a mother.

At a little distance from his van Mr. Balliboy waited, pretending to admire a row of bottles in a wine-merchant's shop window, but, at the same time, keeping an eye upon the woman.

"Was she a thief,—was she come there to steal?" A passing policeman, with a fine military strut, evidently thought so.

"Don't stand about here," he shouted. "Go along home with you!"

The policeman seized her roughly.

"I am doing no harm," the woman said, looking at the name again, "I am only waiting for Mr. Balliboy."

"Go along, you lying drab," grumbled the policeman.

He would have pushed her along, only Mr. Balliboy, who had heard his

name mentioned, came nearer.

"Ain't 'ee poor Mary," he asked, "who was to have married the carpenter at Shelton?"

The policeman winked twice at Mr. Balliboy, smiled and walked on.

"What was it," asked Mr. Balliboy, kindly, as soon as the policeman was out of hearing, "that made 'ee wish to study and remember the name of a poor carrier?"

"I wished to ask you," said the young woman, "whether you would take me as far as the 'Norbury Arms.' Here is my fare," and she handed Mr. Balliboy a shilling—the price of the cross.

Mr. Balliboy put the shilling into his pocket.

"Get up into van," he said, "and 'tis to be hoped they t'others won't mind 'ee."

That day the most respectable of the people of the village had come to town in Mr. Balliboy's van. There was even rich Mrs. Told, clad in warm furs, whose own motor-car had met with an accident the day before. There were others too, as comfortably off,—Mrs. Potten and Mrs. Biggs—and none of these, or even his lesser customers, did Mr. Balliboy wish to offend. He looked anxiously up the street and then into the van.

The young woman's clothes were rags, her toes peeped from her shoes, and she sighed woefully.

Mr. Balliboy gave her a rug to cover her. "Keep tight hold of 'en," he said, "for t'other women be grabbers."

The change in the town from joy to trouble had caused the women who had journeyed with Mr. Balliboy that day to arrive at the van a little late, and in no very good tempers. And, when they did come, they were not best pleased to see a poor woman—worse clothed than a tramp—sitting in the best seat in the van, with her knees covered by Mr. Balliboy's rug.

" 'Tis only Mary," said Mr. Balliboy, hoping to put them at their ease. " 'Tis only this poor toad."

"Mary, is it?" cried Mrs. Biggs angrily, "who did deceive Joseph with her wickedness. What lady would ride with her? Turn her out at once, Mr. Balliboy,—the horrid wretch."

"Out with her!" cried Mrs. Told. "Just look at her," and she whispered unpleasant words to Mrs. Potten.

Mr. Balliboy hesitated. He hardly knew what to do . He had more than once borrowed a little straw from Mrs. Told's stackyard and now he did not want to offend her.

He had a mind to order Mary out, only—putting his hand under his coat to look at his watch—he felt the Christmas present that he had purchased—the cardboard cross.

"Thee needn't sit beside her," he said coaxingly to Mrs. Told, "though she's as clean as any lamb."

"We won't have no lousy breeding beggar with we," shouted Mrs. Biggs, who had taken a little too much to drink at the tavern.

"Let she alone," said Mr. Balliboy, scratching his head and wondering what he

Nativity
L. Vernansal

had better do.

"Thrust her out," cried Mrs. Potten, and, climbing into the van, she spat at the woman.

"Out with her," screamed Mrs. Told "Away with her, away with her!" cried all the women.

"We'll go to John Hawkins; he'll take us home," said Mrs. Told angrily.

Mr. Balliboy winced. He knew how glad his rival would be to welcome all his company.

"Why, what evil has she done?" Mr. Balliboy asked in a milder tone.

With one accord the women shouted out Mary's sorrow.

"Away with her, away with her!" they called.

Mr. Balliboy put his hand into his coat, but it was not his watch hat he felt for this time,—it was his Christmas gift.

"Away with your own selves," he said stoutly. "This maiden be going wi' I, for 'tis me own van."

Mr. Balliboy took his seat angrily and the women left him. He knew that what had happened that afternoon was likely to have a lasting effect upon his future. Everyone in the village would side with the women with whom he had quarreled, and the story of his kindness to Mary would not lose in the telling.

But, before very long, an accident happened that troubled Mr. Balliboy even more than the loss of his customers.—In the middle of a long and lonely road his van broke down.

Mr. Balliboy tried to start the car, but with no success. Other carriers passed by, amongst whom was John Hawkins, and many were the taunts and unseemly jests shouted at him by the Christmas revelers who sat therein.—But soon all was silence, and the road was utterly deserted, for the time was near midnight.

For some while Mr. Balliboy busied himself with the aid of the car lamps, trying to start the engine. But, all at once and without any warning, the lamps went out.

Mr. Balliboy shivered. The weather was changed, a sharp frost had set in and the stars shone brightly. Someone groaned. Mary's pains had come upon her.

"I be going," said Mr. Balliboy, "to get some help for 'ee."

Mr. Balliboy had noticed a little cottage across the moor, with a light in the window. He hurried there, but before he reached the cottage the light had vanished, and, knock as he would at the door, no one replied.

"What be I to do?" cried Mr. Balliboy anxiously, and looked up at the sky.—A large and brightly shining star appeared exactly above his van.

Mr. Balliboy looked at his van and rubbed his eyes. The van was lit up and beams of strange light seemed to emanate from it.

" 'Tain't on fire, I do hope," said Mr. Balliboy. He began to run and came quickly to the car.

Mary was now resting comfortably, while two shining creatures with white wings leaned over her. Upon her lap was her newborn babe, smiling happily.

Mr. Balliboy fumbled in his coat for his Christmas gift. He stepped into the van and held out the cross to the babe.

Mary looked proudly at her infant, and the babe, delighted with the shining toy, took hold of the cross.

The angels wept.

"Though I speak with the tongues of men
and of angels, and have not charity,
I am become as sounding brass,
or a tinkling cymbal. . . .
And now abideth faith, hope, charity,
these three;
but the greatest of these
is charity."

I Corinthians 13:1,13

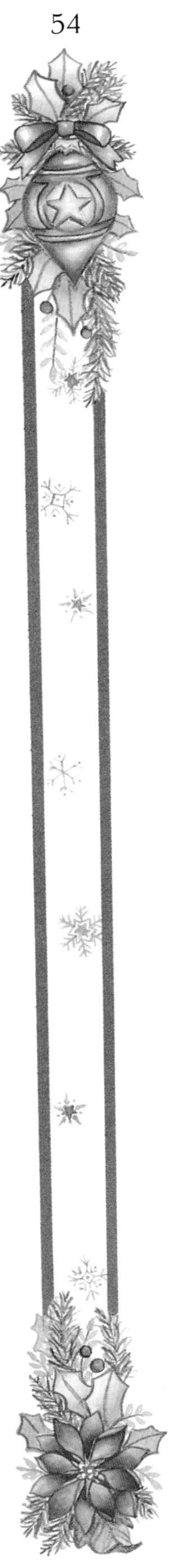

The New Picture Book
Unknown Nineteenth-Century Artist

The Ballad of the Harp-Weaver

Edna St. Vincent Millay

"Son," said my mother,
  When I was knee-high,
"You've need of clothes to cover you,
  And not a rag have I.

"There's nothing in the house
  To make a boy breeches,
Nor shears to cut a cloth with,
  Nor thread to take stitches.

"There's nothing in the house
  But a loaf-end of rye,
And a harp with a woman's head
  Nobody will buy,"
  And she began to cry.

That was in the early fall.
  When came the late fall,
"Son," she said, "the sight of you
  Makes your mother's blood crawl,—

"Little skinny shoulder-blades
  Sticking through your clothes!
And where you'll get a jacket from
  God above knows.

"It's lucky for me, lad,
  Your daddy's in the ground,
And can't see the way I let
  His son go around!"
  And she made a queer sound.

That was in the late fall.
  When the winter came,

I'd not a pair of breeches
Nor a shirt to my name.

I couldn't go to school,
Or out of doors to play.
And all the other little boys
Passes our way.

"Son," said my mother,
"Come, climb into my lap,
And I'll chafe your little bones
While you take a nap."

And, oh, but we were silly
For half an hour or more,
Me with my long legs
Dragging on the floor,

A-rock-rock-rocking
To a mother-goose rhyme!
Oh, but we were happy
For half an hour's time!

But there was I, a great boy,
And what would folks say
To hear my mother singing me
To sleep all day,
In such a daft way?

Men say the winter
Was bad that year;
Fuel was scarce,
And food was dear.

A wind with a wolf's head
Howled about our door,
And we burned up the chairs
And sat upon the floor.

All that was left us
Was a chair we couldn't break,
And the harp with a woman's head
Nobody would take,
For song or pity's sake.

The night before Christmas
I cried with the cold,
I cried myself to sleep
Like a two-year-old.

And in the deep night
I felt my mother rise,
And stare down upon me
With love in her eyes.

I saw my mother sitting
On the one good chair,
A light falling on her
From I couldn't tell where,

Looking nineteen,
And not a day older,
And the harp with a woman's head
Leaned against her shoulder.

Her thin fingers, moving
In the thin, tall strings,
Were weave-weave-weaving
Wonderful things.

Many bright threads,
From where I couldn't see,
Were running through the harp-strings
Rapidly, And gold threads whistling
Through my mother's hand.
I saw the web grow,
And the pattern expand.

She wove a child's jacket,
And when it was done
She laid it on the floor
And wove another one.

She wove a red cloak
So regal to see,
"She's made it for a king's son,"
I said, "and not for me."
But I knew it was for me.

She wove a pair of breeches
Quicker than that!
She wove a pair of boots
And a little cocked hat.

She wove a pair of mittens,
She wove a little blouse,
She wove all night
In the still, cold house.

She sang as she worked,
And the harp-strings spoke;
Her voice never faltered,
And the thread never broke.
And when I awoke,—

There sat my mother
With the harp against her shoulder,
Looking nineteen,
And not a day older,

A smile about her lips,
And a light about her head,
And her hands in the harp-strings
Frozen dead.

And piled up beside her
And toppling to the skies,
Were the clothes of a king's son,
Just my size.

A Christmas Story

Katherine Anne Porter

When she was five years old, my niece asked me again why we celebrated Christmas. She had asked when she was three and when she was four, and each time had listened with a shining, believing face, learning the songs and gazing enchanted at the pictures which I displayed as proof of my stories. Nothing could have been more successful, so I began once more confidently to recite in effect the following:

The feast in the beginning was meant to celebrate with joy the birth of a Child, an event of such importance to this world that angels sang from the skies in human language to announce it and even, if we may believe the old painters, came down with garlands in their hands and danced on the broken roof of the cattle shed where He was born.

"Poor baby," she said, disregarding the angels, "didn't His papa and mama have a house?"

They weren't quite so poor as all that, I went on, slightly dashed, for last year the angels had been the center of interest. His papa and mama were able to pay taxes at least, but they had to leave home and go to Bethlehem to pay them, and they could have afforded a room at the inn, but the town was crowded because everybody came to pay taxes at the same time. They were quite lucky to find a manger full of clean straw to sleep in. When the baby was born, a goodhearted servant girl named Bertha came to help the mother. Bertha had no arms, but in that moment she unexpectedly grew a fine new pair of arms and hands, and the first thing she did with them was to wrap the baby in swaddling clothes. We then sang together the song about Bertha the armless servant. Thinking I saw a practical question dawning in a pure blue eye, I hurried on to the part about how all the animals—cows, calves, donkeys, sheep . . .

"And pigs?"

Pigs perhaps even had knelt in a ring around the baby and breathed upon Him to keep Him warm through His first hours in this world. A new star appeared and moved in a straight course toward Bethlehem for many nights to guide three kings who came from far countries to place important gifts in the straw beside Him: gold, frankincense and myrrh.

"What beautiful clothes," said the little girl, looking at the picture of Charles the Seventh of France kneeling before a meek blond girl and a charming baby.

It was the way some people used to dress. The Child's mother, Mary, and His father, Joseph, a carpenter, were such unworldly simple souls they never

once thought of taking any honor to themselves nor of turning the gifts to their own benefit.

"What became of the gifts?" asked the little girl.

Nobody knows, nobody seems to have paid much attention to them, they were never heard of again after that night. So far as we know, those were the only presents anyone ever gave to the Child while He lived. But He was not unhappy. Once He caused a cherry tree in full fruit to bend down one of his branches so His mother could more easily pick cherries. We then sang about the cherry tree until we came to the words: "Then up spake old Joseph, so rude and unkind."

"Why was he so unkind?"

Christmas Shopping
Eugene Galien Laloue, 1854-1941
Courtesy Adam Levene, Albourne

I thought perhaps he was just in a cross mood.

"What was he cross about?"

Dear me, what should I say now? After all, this was not my daughter, whatever would her mother answer to this? I asked her in turn what she was cross about when she was cross? She couldn't remember ever having been cross but was willing to let the subject pass. We moved on to The Withy Tree, which tells how the Child once a bridge of sunbeams over a stream and crossed upon it, and played a trick on John the Baptist, who followed Him, by removing the beams and letting John fall in the water. The Child's mother switched Him smartly for this with a branch of withy, and the Child shed loud tears and wished bad luck upon the whole race of withies for ever.

"What's a withy?" asked the little girl. I looked it up in the dictionary and discovered it meant osier, or willows.

"Just a willow like ours?" she asked, rejecting this intrusion of the commonplace. Yes, but once, when His father was struggling with a heavy piece of timber almost beyond his strength, the Child ran and touched it with one finger and the timber rose and fell properly into place. At night His mother cradled Him in a far place; and the Child, moved by her tears, spoke long before it was time for Him to speak and His first words were, "Don't be sad, for you shall be Queen of Heaven." And there she was in an old picture, with the airy jeweled crown being set upon her golden hair.

I thought how nearly all of these tender medieval songs and legends about this Child were concerned with trees, wood, timbers, beams, crosspieces; and even the pagan north transformed its great tree festooned with human entrails into a blithe festival tree hung with gifts for the Child, and some savage old man of the woods became a rollicking saint with a big belly. But I had never talked about Santa Claus, because myself I had not liked from the first, and did not even then approve of the boisterous way he had almost crowded out the Child from His own birthday feast.

"I like the part about the sunbeam bridge the best," said the little girl, and then she told me she had a dollar of her own and would I take her to buy a Christmas present for her mother.

We wandered from shop to shop, and I admired the way the little girl, surrounded by tons of seductive, specially manufactured holiday merchandise for children, kept her attention fixed resolutely on objects appropriate to the grown-up world. She considered seriously in turn a silver tea service, one thousand dollars; an embroidered handkerchief with lace on it, five dollars; a dressing-table mirror framed in porcelain flowers, eighty-five dollars; a preposterously showy crystal flask of perfume, one-hundred-twenty dollars; a gadget for curling the eyelashes, seventy-five cents; a large plaque of colored glass jewelry, thirty dollars; a cigarette case of some fraudulent material, two dollars and fifty cents. She weakened, but only for a moment, before a mechanical monkey with real fur who did calisthenics on a crossbar if you wound him up, one dollar and ninety-eight cents.

The prices of these objects did not influence their relative value to her and bore no connection whatever to the dollar she carried in her hand. Our shopping had also no connection with the birthday of the Child or the legends and pictures. Her air of reserve toward the long series of blear-eyed, shapeless old men wearing red flannel blouses and false, white-wool whiskers said all too plainly that they in no way fulfilled her notions of Christmas merriment. She shook hands with all of them politely, could not be persuaded to ask for anything from them and seemed not to question the obvious spectacle of thousands of persons everywhere buying presents instead of waiting for one of the army of Santa Clauses to bring them, as they all so profusely promised.

Christmas is what we make it and this is what we have so cynically made of it: not the feast of the Child in the straw-filled crib, nor even the homely winter bounty of the old pagan with the reindeer, but a great glittering commercial fair, gay enough with music and food and extravagance of feeling and behavior and expense, more and more on the order of the ancient Saturnalia. I have nothing against Saturnalia, it belongs to this season of the year: but how do we get so confused about the true meaning of even our simplest-appearing pastimes?

Meanwhile, for our money we found a present for the little girl's mother. It turned out to be a small green pottery shell with a colored bird perched on the rim which the little girl took for an ash tray, which it may as well have been.

"We'll wrap it up and hang it on the tree and say it came from Santa Claus," she said, trustfully making of me a fellow conspirator.

"You don't believe in Santa Claus any more?" I asked carefully, for we had taken her credulity for granted. I had already seen in her face that morning a skeptical view of my sentimental legends, she was plainly trying to sort out one thing from another in them; and I was turning over in my mind the notion of beginning again with her on other grounds, of making an attempt to draw, however faintly, some boundary lines between fact and fancy, which is not so difficult; but also further to show where truth and poetry were, if not the same being, at least twins who could wear each other's clothes. But that couldn't be done in a day nor with pedantic intention. I was perfectly prepared for the first half of her answer, but the second took me by surprise.

"No, I don't," she said, with the freedom of her natural candor, "but please don't tell my mother, for she still does."

For herself, then, she rejected the gigantic hoax which a whole powerful society had organized and was sustaining at the vastest pains and expense, and she was yet to find the grain of truth lying lost in the gaudy debris around her, but there remained her immediate human situation, and that she could deal with, or so she believed: her mother believed in Santa Claus, or she would not have said so. The little girl did not believe in what her mother had told her, she did not want her mother to know she did not believe, yet her mother's illusions must not be disturbed. In that moment of decision her infancy was gone forever, it had vanished there before my eyes.

Very thoughtfully I took the hand of my budding little diplomat, whom we had so lovingly, unconsciously prepared for her career, which no doubt would be quite a successful one; and we walked along in the bright sweet-smelling Christmas dusk, myself for once completely silenced.

O Holy Night
Adolphe Adam
Adolphe Adam
1. O ho-ly Night!_ the stars are bright-ly
shin - - ing, It is the night of the dear Sa-viour's
birth. Long lay the world_ in sin and er-ror
pin - - ing, Till He ap-peared and the spir - it felt its
pp
worth. A thrill of hope the wea-ry world re-joic - es, For
yon-der breaks_ a new and glo - rious morn._

Fall on your knees! Oh, hear the an-gel
voic - es! O night di - vine, the
night when Christ was born; O night, O
ho - ly night, O night di - vine!

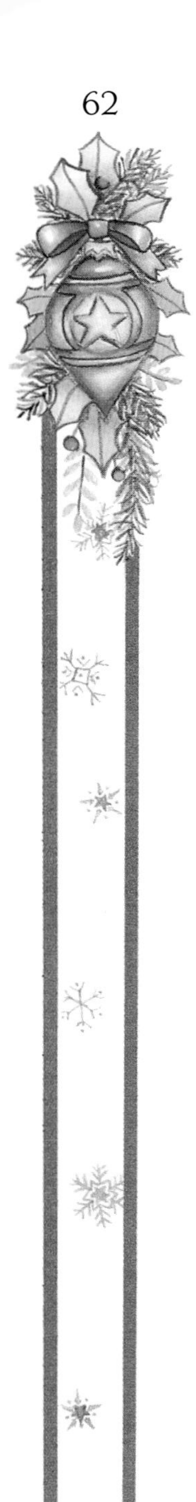

The Holy Night

Selma Lagerlof

There was a man who went out in the dark night to borrow live coals to kindle a fire. He went from hut to hut and knocked. "Dear friends, help me!" said he. "My wife has just given birth to a child, and I must make a fire to warm her and the little one."

But it was way in the night, and all the people were asleep. No one replied.

The man walked and walked. At last he saw the gleam of a fire a long way off. Then he went in that direction, and saw that the fire was burning in the open. A lot of sheep were sleeping around the fire, and an old shepherd sat and watched over the flock.

When the man who wanted to borrow fire came up to the sheep, he saw that three big dogs lay asleep at the shepherd's feet. All three awoke when the man approached and opened their great jaws, as though they wanted to bark; but not a sound was heard. The man noticed that the hair on their backs stood up and that their sharp, white teeth glistened in the firelight. They dashed toward him. He felt that one of them bit at his leg and one at his hand and that one clung to his throat. But their jaws and teeth wouldn't obey them, and the man didn't suffer the least harm.

Now the man wished to go farther, to get what he needed. But the sheep lay back to back and so close to one another that he couldn't pass them. Then the man stepped upon their backs and walked over them and up to the fire. And not one of the animals awoke or moved.

When the man had almost reached the fire, the shepherd looked up. He was a surly old man, who was unfriendly and harsh toward human beings. And when he saw the strange man coming, he seized the long spiked staff, which he always held in his hand when he tended his flock, and threw it at him. The staff came right toward the man, but, before it reached him, it turned off to one side and whizzed past him, far out in the meadow.

Now the man came up to the shepherd and said to him: "Good man, help me, and lend me a little fire! My wife has just given birth to a child, and I must make a fire to warm her and the little one."

The shepherd would rather have said no, but when he pondered that the dogs couldn't hurt the man, and the sheep had not run from him, and that the staff had not wished to strike him, he was a little afraid, and dared not deny the man that which he asked.

"Take as much as you need!" he said to the man.

But then the fire was nearly burnt out. There were no logs or branches left, only a big heap of live coals; and the stranger had neither spade nor shovel, wherein he could carry the red-hot coals.

When the shepherd saw this, he said again: "Take as much as you need!" And he was glad that the man wouldn't be able to take away any coals.

But the man stooped and picked coals from the ashes with his bare hands, and laid them in his mantle. And he didn't burn his hands when he touched them, nor did the coals scorch his mantle; but he carried them away as if they had been nuts or apples.

And when the shepherd, who was such a cruel and hardhearted man, saw all this, he began to wonder to himself: "What kind of a night is this, when the dogs do not bite, the sheep are not scared, the staff does not kill, or the fire scorch?" He called the stranger back, and said to him: "What kind of a night is this? And how does it happen

that all things show you compassion?"

Then said the man: "I cannot tell you if you yourself do not see it." And he wished to go his way, that he might soon make a fire and warm his wife and child.

But the shepherd did not wish to lose sight of the man before he had found out what all this might portend. He got up and followed the man till they came to the place where he lived.

Then the shepherd saw that the man didn't have so much as a hut to dwell in, but that his wife and babe were lying in a mountain grotto, where there was nothing except the cold and naked stone walls.

But the shepherd thought that perhaps the poor innocent child might freeze to death there in the grotto; and, although he was a hard man, he was touched, and thought he would like to help it. And he loosened his knapsack from his shoulder, took from it a soft white sheepskin, gave it to the strange man, and said that he should let the child sleep on it.

But just as soon as he showed that he, too, could be merciful, his eyes were opened, and he saw what he had not been abel to see before and heard what he could not have heard before.

He saw that all around him stood a ring of little silver-winged angels, and each held a stringed instrument, and all sang in loud tones that tonight the Saviour was born who should redeem the world from its sins.

Then he understood how all things were so happy this night that they didn't want to do anything wrong.

And it was not only around the shepherd that there were angels, but he saw them everywhere. They sat inside the grotto, they sat outside on the mountain, and they flew under the heavens. They came marching in great companies, and as they passed, they paused and cast a glance at the child.

There were such jubilation and such gladness and songs and play! And all this he saw in the dark night, whereas before he could not have made out anything. He was so happy because his eyes had been opened that he fell upon his knees and thanked God.

What that shepherd saw, we might also see, for the angels fly down from heaven every Christmas Eve, if we could only see them.

You must remember this, for it is as true, as true as that I see you and you see me. It is not revealed by the light of lamps or candles, and it does not depend upon sun and moon; but that which is needful is that we have such eyes as can see God's glory.

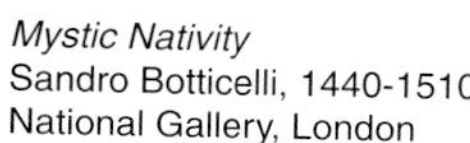

Mystic Nativity
Sandro Botticelli, 1440-1510
National Gallery, London

I Am the Christmas Spirit

E. C. Baird

I am the Christmas spirit!

I enter the home of poverty, causing palefaced children to open their eyes wide, in pleased wonder. I cause the miser's clutched hand to relax, and thus paint a bright spot on his soul.

I cause the aged to renew their youth, and to laugh in the old, glad way.

I keep romance alive in the heart of childhood, and brighten sleep with dreams of woven magic.

I cause eager feet to climb dark stairways with filled baskets, leaving behind hearts amazed at the goodness of the world.

I cause the prodigal to pause a moment on his wild, wasteful way, and send to anxious love some little token that releases glad tears—tears which wash away the hard lines of sorrow.

I enter dark prison cells, reminding scarred manhood of what might have been and pointing forward to good days yet to be.

I come softly into the still, white home of pain, and lips that are too weak to speak just tremble in silent, eloquent gratitude.

In a thousand ways, I cause the weary world to look up into the face of God, and for a little moment forget the things that are small and wretched.

I am the Christmas spirit!

Village at Christmas
Stark, New Hampshire

Christmas Is for Remembering

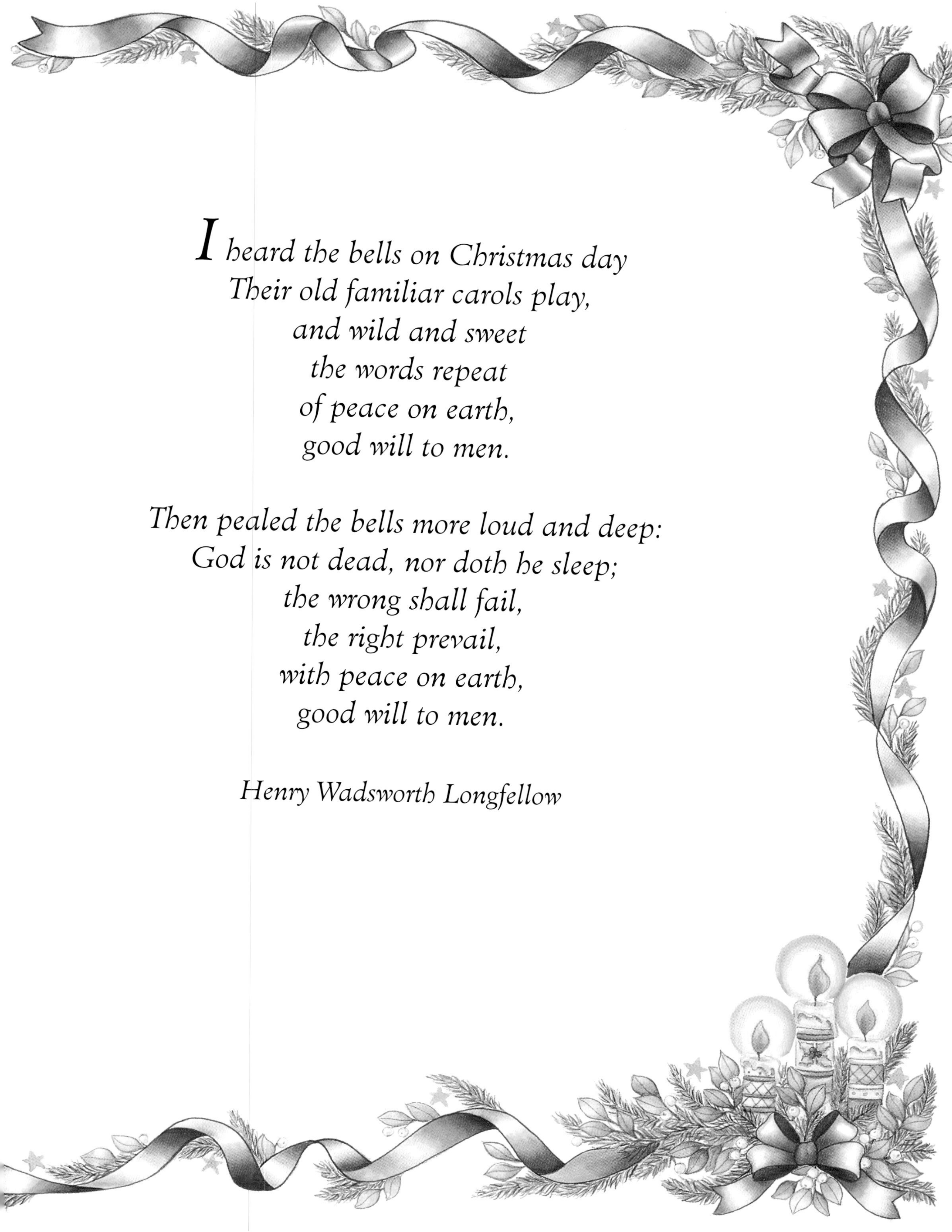

I heard the bells on Christmas day
Their old familiar carols play,
and wild and sweet
the words repeat
of peace on earth,
good will to men.

Then pealed the bells more loud and deep:
God is not dead, nor doth he sleep;
the wrong shall fail,
the right prevail,
with peace on earth,
good will to men.

Henry Wadsworth Longfellow

Christmas Eve in Olden Times

Sir Walter Scott

A Christmas Recital
Friedrich Ortlieb, 1839-1909

And well our Christian sires of old
Loved when the year its course had
roll'd,
And brought blithe Christmas back
again,
With all his hospitable train.
Domestic and religious rite
Gave honour to the holy night:
On Christmas Eve the bells were
rung;
On Christmas Eve the mass was
sung:
That only night in all the year,
Saw the stoled priest the chalice rear.

The damsel donn'd her kirtle sheen;
The hall was dress'd with holly
green;
Forth to the wood did merry
men go,
To gather in the mistletoe.
Then open'd wide the Baron's hall
To vassal, tenant, serf, and all;
Power laid his rod of rule aside,
And Ceremony doffed his pride.

The heir, with roses in his shoes,
That night might village partner
choose.
The lord, underogating, share
The vulgar game of "post and pair."
All hail'd, with uncontroll'd delight,
And general voice, the happy night
That to the cottage, as the crown,
Brought tidings of salvation down!

The fire, with well-dried logs sup
plied,
Went roaring up the chimney wide;
The huge hall-table's oaken face,
Scrubb'd till it shone, the day to
grace
Bore them upon its massive board
No mark to part the squire and lord.

Then was brought in the lusty brawn
By old blue-coated serving man;
Then the grim boar's head frowned
on high,
Crested with bays and rosemary
Well can the green-garbed ranger tell
How, when, and where the monster
fell;
What dogs before his death he tore,
And all the baiting of the boar.

The wassail round in good brown
bowls,
Garnish'd with ribbons, blithely
trowls.
There the huge sirloin reek'd; hard
by
Plum-porridge stood, and
Christmas-pye;
Nor fail'd old Scotland to produce,
At such high tide, her savory goose.
Then came the merry masquers in,
And carols roar'd with blithesome
din

If unmelodious was the song,
It was a hearty note, and strong.
Who list may in their mumming see
Traces of ancient mystery;
White shirts supplied the
masquerade,
And smutted cheeks the visors
made;
But oh! what masquers, richly dight,
Can boast of bosoms half so light!

England was merry England when
Old Christmas brought his sports
again.
'Twas Christmas broached the
mightiest ale,
'Twas Christmas told the merriest
tale;
A Christmas gambol oft could cheer
The poor man's heart through half
the year.

A Country Parson's Christmas Eve

Written in 1870-1879 by Rev. Francis Kilvert

Writing Christmas letters all the morning. In the afternoon I went to the church with Dora and Teddy to put up Christmas decorations. Dora had been very busy for some days past making the straw letters for the Christmas text. Fair Rosamund and good Elizabeth Knight came to the church to help us and worked heartily and well. They had made some pretty ivy knots and bunches for the pulpit panels and the ivy blossoms cleverly whitened with flour looked just like white flowers.

The churchwarden Jacob Knight was sitting by his sister in front of the roaring fire. We were talking of the death of Major Torrens on the ice at Corsham pond yesterday. Speaking of people slipping and falling on ice the good churchwarden sagely remarked, "Some do fall on their faces and some do fall on their rumps. And they as do hold their selves uncommon stiff do most in generally fall on their rumps."

I took old John Bryant a Christmas packet of tea and sugar and raisins from my mother. The old man had covered himself almost entirely over in his bed to keep himself warm, like a marmot in its nest. He said, "If I live till New Year's Day I shall have seen ninety-six New Years." He said also, "I do often see things flying about me, thousands and thousands of them about half the size of a large pea, and they are red, white, blue, and yellow and all colors". I asked Mr. Morgan what they were and he said they were the spirits of just men made perfect.

Father Christmas
E. F. Skinner

Christmas at Claremont

from Queen Victoria's Journal, December 24, 1836

I awoke after 7 and got up at 8. After 9 breakfasted, at a little after 10 we left Kensington with dearest Lehzen, Lady Conroy and—Dashy and reached Claremont at a quarter to 12. Played and sang. At 2 dearest Lehzen, Victoire and I went out, and came home at 20 minutes past 8. No one was stirring about the gipsy encampment except George, which I was sorry for as I was anxious to know how our poor friends were, after this bitterly cold night. Played and sang.

Received from dearest, best Lehzen, as a Christmas box two lovely little Dresden China figures, two pair of lovely little chased gold buttons, a small lovely button with an angel's head which she used to wear herself, and a pretty music book; from good Louis a beautiful piece of Persian stuff for an album; and from Victoire and Emily Gardiner a small box worked by themselves. Wrote my journal, went down to arrange Mamma's table for her. At 6 we dined. Mr. Edward Byrne and Mr. Conroy stayed here. Mr. Byne is going to stay here a night or two. Very soon after dinner Mamma sent for us into the gallery, where all the things were arranged on different tables.

From my dear Mamma I received a beautiful massive gold buckle in the shape of two serpents; a lovely little delicate gold chain with turquoise clasp; a lovely coloured sketch of dearest Aunt Louise by Partridge copied from the picture he brought and so like her; 3 beautiful drawings by Munn, one lovely seaview by Peser and one cattle piece by Cooper (all coloured), 3 prints, a book called Finden's Tableau, Heath's Picturesque Annual, Ireland; both these are very pretty; Friendship's offering and the English Annual for 1837, the Holy Land illustrated beautifully, two handkerchiefs, a very pretty black satin apron trimmed with red velvet, and two almanacks. I am very thankful to my dear Mamma for all these very pretty things.

From dear Uncle Leopold a beautiful turquoise ring; from the Queen a fine piece of Indian gold tissue, and from Sir J. Conroy a print. I gave my dear Lehzen a green morocco jewel case, and the Picturesque Annual; Mamma gave her a shawl, pair of turquoise earrings, an annual, and handkerchiefs. I then took Mamma to the Library where my humble table was arranged; I gave her a bracelet made of my hair, and the Keepsake, and Oriental Annual.

I stayed up til eleven!

Memory Clings to These

Edgar A. Guest

There used to be a sideboard,
in the days when I was small,
Which with tasty things was loaded
for the friends who came to call.
There were little pies of mincemeat
and a plate of lemon tarts,
Which in England are the custom
when the Christmas season starts.
There were almonds mixed with raisins;
There were cookies for the children,
always frosted red and white.

It is strange what memory clings to—
The plum pudding always came
To the table decked with holly
and for Christmas Day aflame.
With an apple in its mouth
was a roasted suckling pig,
Which for mother's finest platter
was a little bit too gib.
And my father, I remember,
seemed the happiest of men
As he stood to do the carving
for his family back then.

Oh, the years are long and many
since my parents went away,
But I always feel their presence
very close on Christmas Day.
And I always see the sideboard
with its pie and cookie trays,
And the almonds and the raisins
and the pudding set ablaze.
I was just little fellow,
but tenaciously I hold
To the wonder and the gladness
of those Christmas days of old.

Wood-burning Kitchen Stove at Christmastime

It Came upon the Midnight Clear
Edmund H. Sears
Richard S. Willis
p
It came up-on the mid-night clear, That glo-rious song of old, From
mf
an-gels bend-ing near the earth, To touch their harps of gold: "Peace
pp
on the earth, good-will to men From heav'n's all gra-cious King," The

Still through the cloven skies they come,
With peaceful wings unfurl'd,
And still their heav'nly music floats
O'er all the weary world:
Above its sad and lowly plains
They bend on hov'ring wing.
And ever o'er its Babel sounds
The blessed angels sing.

O ye, beneath life's crushing load,
Whose forms are bending low,
Who toil along the climbing way
With painful steps and slow:
Look now, for glad and golden hours
Come swiftly on the wing
Oh rest beside the weary road
And hear the angels sing.

For lo! the days are hast'ning on,
By prophets seen of old,
When with the ver circling years,
Shall come the time foretold,
When the new heav'n and earth shall own
The Prince of Peace their King,
And the whole world send back the song
Which now the angels sing.

For weeks before Christmas the spirit was in the air – Willie and I – that's your Uncle Bill – were good as we could be. He would keep the wood box in the kitchen heaped high with cord wood – and I would help mamma clear the table, wash and dry the dishes.

Then we would do our home work and help make gifts for Christmas. Mamma would make pink, silk covered, padded coat hangers with pretty little bows – and crocheted table pieces and knitted wristlets – and for daddy she would always make a pair of silk elastic sleeve supporters – with pretty pink ribbon bows for each arm. Willie and I would bring our painting sets home from school and paint pieces of cardboard and paste pretty pictures on them. It was a lot of fun because most everyone *MADE* their Christmas gifts – there were very few boughten ones in those days. Yes, it was a lot different – yesterday – and kinda nice too.

When the clock on the mantel would strike half past eight - Willie and I were hustled off to bed. Just before we went upstairs, daddy would read to us about the first Christmas - from St. Luke and Matthew - in the bible. Then we'd quickly say our prayers at mamma's knee - and then go to bed.

They were big fluffy beds - with feather ticks and feather comforters. On real cold nights, Mamma would wrap a hot sad iron in a piece of flannel and would put it in our bed at our feet and soon we would be sound asleep - dreaming dreams about Christmas.

Even on our way to school there was happy talk about Christmas doings at everyone's house - and the gifts that were being made. In school - for weeks before - we would sing all the old Christmas carols and recite Christmas poems - getting ready for the Christmas exercises.

And at Sunday school it was the same thing. We would sing all the beautiful Christmas songs - and rehearse the Story of the Nativity over and over again. Willie was a shepherd - and one year I played the part of Mary - I will never forget the warm glowing feeling - and the tears in mamma's eyes - when I tenderly showed my doll in the crib to the Shepherds.

A few days before Christmas, daddy would let Willie and me go with him to pick out our tree for Christmas. We didn't buy them on the corner those days – we would go out in the woods and chop one down.

Christmas Eve came at last – with big white snow flakes in the air – and the bells on the sleighs would jingle jingle – you could hear them for miles in the clear cold air.

Right after supper we all bundled up and walked to church services. Christmas was never so beautiful – everyone so gay and happy – the church was aglow with candles and Christmas decorations – and there was the manger setting – where our play "The Story of the Nativity" would be presented.

Oh! – Christmas Eve was a happy, busy time.
When we returned home from church – we hung
our stockings over the fireplace – placed a couple
pieces of brown sugar on a plate for Santa's
reindeer and a piece of cake for Santa –
said a very special prayer that night –
and in our excitement to go to bed
– we forgot our hot iron.
S
We quivered with excitement – as we listened with strained ears
to all the unusual sounds we heard that night. We KNEW we
could hear Santa's reindeer on the roof – and Santa talking in
muffled tones to his brownies who were helping him.
Finally we drifted off to slumberland – and when we heard daddy
shake the grates in the kitchen stove – we knew Christmas
morning was here at last!

We raced downstairs – still in our flannel nightgowns – and – lo and behold! – the most wonderful – beautiful – thrilling sight in our lives – was our gorgeous tree all trimmed with colored paper chains – stringed popcorn – and shining doodads – and a big glistening star right on top – with a million colored candles carefully clipped at the end of every branch –

And Willie was busy admiring his brand new pair of clamp-on skates – a new knit stocking cap – mittens – a magic lantern – and a brand new pair of brown leather boots with bright copper toes.

And there beneath the tree was the very same little cast iron cooking stove I had looked at in the store window so many times. It was just like mamma's – And there was a real store boughten girl's sled with swan's head runners – bright red mittens – a green scarf – new stockings – and my oh my – a brand new pair of high buttoned shiny patent leather shoes for Sunday.

God
And our stockings – Santa was certainly
wonderful to us – in the toe of each stocking
was a real orange – and nuts and apples –
and a tin horn – and some hard ribbon candy –
and some peppermint canes –
It was wonderful!

Yuletide in a Younger World

Thomas Hardy

We believed in highdays then,
    And could glimpse at night
        On Christmas Eve
Imminent oncomings of radiant revel—
    Doings of delight:—
        Now we have no such sight.

We had eyes for phantoms then,
    And at bridge or stile
        On Christmas Eve
Clear beheld those countless ones who had crossed it
    Crossed again in file:—
        Such has ceased longwhile!

We liked divination then,
    And, as they homeward wound
        On Christmas Eve
We could read men's dreams within them spinning
    Even as wheels spin round:—
        Now we are blinker-bound.

We heard still small voices then,
    And, in the dim serene
        On Christmas Eve,
Caught the far-times tones of fire-filled prophets
    Long on earth unseen . . .
        Can such ever have been?

Church and Village in Winter
Hebron, New Hampshire

Christmas Is for Children

Why do bells of Christmas ring?
Why do little children sing?

Once a lovely shining star,
Seen by shepherds from afar,
Gently moved until its light
Made a manger's cradle bright.

There a darling baby lay
Pillowed soft upon the hay;
And its mother sang and smiled:
"This is Christ, the Holy Child!"

Therefore bells for Christmas ring,
Therefore little children sing.

Eugene Field

Holly-Crowned Father Christmas with Child
Unknown Nineteenth-Century Artist

Is There a Santa Claus?

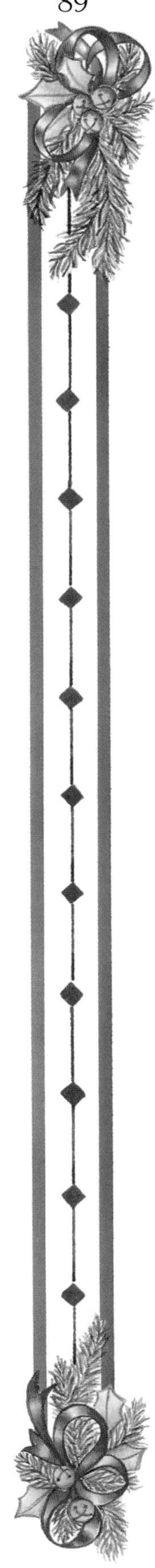

We take pleasure in answering at once and thus prominently the communication below, expressing at the same time our great gratification that its faithful author is numbered among the friends of *The Sun*:

> Dear Editor, I am 8 years old.
> Some of my little friends say there is no Santa Claus.
> Papa says "If you see it in The Sun it's so."
> Please tell me the truth. Is there a Santa Claus?
>
> Virginia O'Hanlon
> 1115 West Ninety-fifth Street

Virginia, your little friends are wrong. They have been affected by the skepticism of a skeptical age. They do not believe except they see. They think that nothing can be which is not comprehensible by their little minds. All minds, Virginia, whether they be men's or children's, are little. In this great universe of ours man is a mere insect, an ant, in his intellect, as compared with the boundless world about him, as measured by the intelligence capable of grasping the whole of truth and knowledge.

Yes, Virginia, there is a Santa Claus. He exists as certainly as love and generosity and devotion exist, and you know that they abound and give to your life its highest beauty and joy. Alas! how dreary would be the world if there were no Santa Claus! It would be as dreary as if there were no Virginias. There would be no childlike faith then, no poetry, no romance to make tolerable this existence. We should have no enjoyment, except in sense and sight. The eternal light with which childhood fills the world would be extinguished.

Not believe in Santa Claus! You might as well not believe in fairies! You might get your papa to hire men to watch in all the chimneys on Christmas Eve to catch Santa Claus, but even if they did not see Santa Claus coming down what would that prove? Nobody sees Santa Claus but that is no sign that there is no Santa Claus. The most real things in the world are those that neither children nor men can see. Did you ever see fairies dancing on the lawn? Of course not, but that's no proof that they are not there. Nobody can conceive or imagine all the wonders there are unseen and unseeable in the world.

You tear apart the baby's rattle and see what makes the noise inside, but there is a veil covering the unseen world which not the strongest man, not even the united strength of all the strongest men that ever lived, could tear apart. Only faith, fancy, poetry, love, romance, can push aside that curtain and view and picture the supernal beauty and glory beyond. Is it all real? Ah, Virginia, in all this world there is nothing else real and abiding.

No Santa Claus! Thank God! he lives, and he lives forever. A thousand years from now, Virginia, nay, ten times ten thousand years from now, he will continue to make glad the heart of childhood.

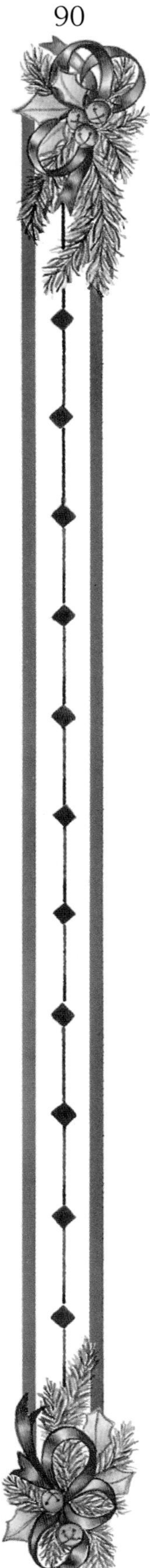

The Little Match Girl

Hans Christian Andersen

A long, long time ago on a bitter cold New Year's Eve, a poor little girl with bare feet was trudging along through the cold deep snow. Yes, her feet were bare because she had no real shoes and the large slippers someone had given her had been lost when she ran to get out of the way of a cart, and a naughty boy ran away with one of them. So she was walking in the bitter, bitter cold snow and her poor little bare feet were red and blue with cold. In her apron she was carrying a lot of matches that she was trying to sell for a penny a box. No one had bought any from her all day long—and the poor little thing was shivering and hungry, but she was afraid to go home because her cruel foster father would beat her—for she had not sold even a half-penny of matches all day long.

She looked into the bright cheerful windows of homes as she walked by. Everyone seemed so warm and comfortable and happy—everyone except the poor little match girl. She saw a beautiful trimmed Christmas tree in one; from another came the tempting aroma of roast goose, and she was so very hungry.

It was getting colder and snowing harder, and it was now real dark. She huddled in a corner between two buildings to try to keep warm. She took one little match from a box and lit it to warm her frozen fingers. How brightly it sputtered; in its light she seemed to see a big warm stove—how warm and cozy it was—but when the match burned out the stove disappeared and she was colder than ever.

She struck a second match and before her was a big table with a glistening white tablecloth. There was a huge roast duck and apples and cake and warm milk and she was so happy because she was so terribly hungry. Then just when she was reaching for the roast duck, the match burned out, and then she was colder and more hungry than ever. She lighted another match and lo! there was the most beautiful Christmas tree she had ever seen—full of shiny toys and sparkling candles, candies, and everything nice. The beautiful candles rose higher and higher until they were only stars in the sky-—then one of them fell.

"That falling star means someone is dying" she said to herself, "my dear grandmother used to tell me that." She quickly lit another match, and another, then a whole hand full—and right in the bright glow—so dazzling and bright, and so kind and loving stood her dear old grandmother with outstretched arms.

"Grandmother!" she cried, "please take me with you! I know you will go away when the match burns out, just like the roast goose and the warm stove and the Christmas tree did." She quickly lighted the whole box of matches—because she did not want her grandmother to go. The matches burned with a blaze that was light as day. Her grandmother had never seemed so beautiful—and as she took the poor little match girl in her arms she flew up with her brightness and joy, high, so very high—and there was no cold and no hunger—and no sorrow—and—no matches to sell—for they were in heaven.

In the morning, people passed by and saw the poor little girl still huddled between the buildings, with burned matches about her.

A Great Undertaking
Unknown Nineteenth-Century Artist

L. L.

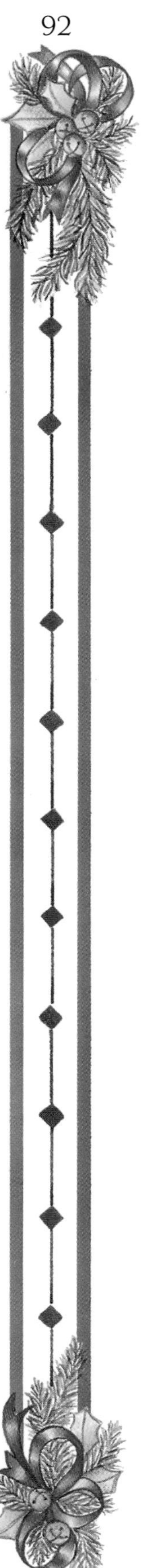

The Duel

Eugene Field

The gingham dog and the calico cat
Side by side on the table sat;
'Twas half-past twelve, and (what do you think!)
Nor one nor t'other had slept a wink!
The old Dutch clock and the Chinese plate
Appeared to know as sure as fate
There was going to be a terrible spat.
(I wasn't there; I simply state
What was told to me by the Chinese plate!)

The gingham dog went "Bow-wow-wow!"
And the calico cat replied "Mee-ow!"
The air was littered, an hour or so,
With bits of gingham and calico,
While the old Dutch clock in the chimney place
Up with its hands before its face,
For it always dreaded a family row!
(Now mind: I'm only telling you
What the old Dutch clock declares is true!)

The Chinese plate looked very blue,
And wailed, "Oh, dear! what shall we do!"
But the gingham dog and the calico cat
Wallowed this way and tumbled that,
Employing every tooth and claw
In the awfullest way you ever saw—
And, oh! how the gingham and calico flew!
(Don't fancy I exaggerate—
I got my news from the Chinese plate!)

Next morning, where the two had sat
They found no trace of dog or cat;
And some folks think unto this day
That burglars stole the pair away!
But the truth about the cat and pup
Is this: They ate each other up!
Now what do you really think of that!
(The old Dutch clock it told me so,
And that is how I came to know.)

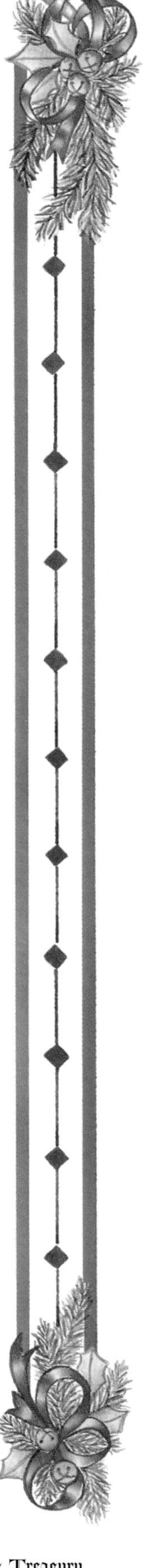

Christmas Fancy Dress Party
Percy Tarrant

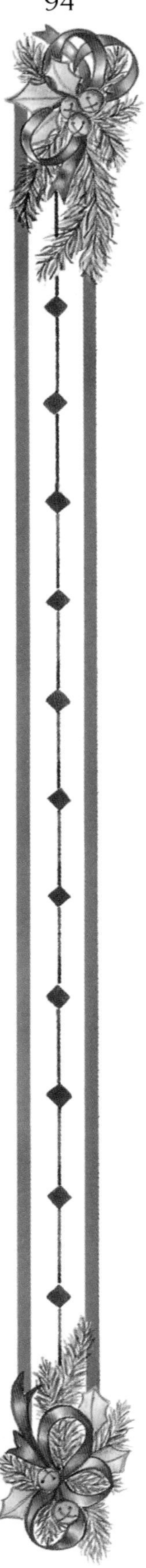

The Peterkins' Christmas Tree

Lucretia Hale

Pretty early in the autumn the Peterkins began to prepare for their Christmas tree. Everything was done in great privacy, as it was to be a surprise to the neighbors, as well as to the rest of the family. Mr. Peterkin had been up to Mr. Bromwich's woodlot, and, with his consent, selected the tree. Agamemnon went to look at it occasionally after dark, and Solomon John made frequent visits to it, mornings, just after sunrise. Mr. Peterkin drove Elizabeth Eliza and her mother that way and pointed furtively to it with his whip, but none of them ever spoke of it aloud to each other. It was suspected that the little boys had been to see it Wednesday and Saturday afternoons. But they came home with their pockets full of chestnuts and said nothing about it.

At length Mr. Peterkin had it cut down and brought secretly into the Larkins' barn. A week or two before Christmas, a measurement was made of it with Elizabeth Eliza's yard measure. To Mr. Peterkin's great dismay, it was discovered that it was too high to stand in the back parlor. This fact was brought out at a secret council of Mr. and Mrs. Peterkin, Elizabeth Eliza, and Agamemnon.

Agamemnon suggested that it might be set up slanting, but Mrs. Peterkin was sure it would make her dizzy, and the candles would drip.

But a brilliant idea came to Mr. Peterkin. He proposed that the ceiling of the parlor should be raised to make room for the top of the tree.

Elizabeth Eliza thought the space would need to be quite large. It must not be like a small box, or you could not see the tree.

"Yes," said Mr. Peterkin, "I should have the ceiling lifted all across the room; the effect would be finer."

Elizabeth Eliza objected to having the whole ceiling raised, because her room was over the back parlor, and she would have no floor while the alteration was going on, which would be very awkward. Besides, her room was not very high now, and if the floor were raised, perhaps she could not walk in it upright.

Mr. Peterkin explained that he didn't propose altering the whole ceiling, but to lift up a ridge across the room at the back part where the tree was to stand. This would make a hump, to be sure, in Elizabeth Eliza's room, but it would go across the whole room.

Elizabeth Eliza said she would not mind that. It would be like the cuddly thing that comes up on the deck of a ship, that you sit against, only here you would not have the seasickness. She thought she should like it for a rarity. She might use it for a divan.

Mrs. Peterkin thought it would come in the worn place in the carpet, and might be a convenience in making the carpet over.

Agamemnon was afraid there would be trouble in keeping the matter secret, for it would be a long piece of work for a carpenter; but Mr. Peterkin proposed having the carpenter for a day or two, for a number of other jobs.

The carpenter, however, insisted that the tree could be cut off at the lower end to suit the height of the parlor and demurred at so great a change as altering the ceiling. But Mr. Peterkin had set his mind upon the improvement, and Eliza-

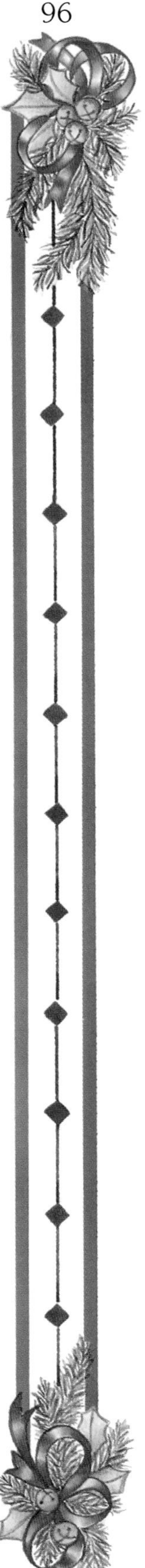

beth Eliza had cut her carpet in preparation for it.

So the folding doors into the back parlor were closed, and for nearly a fortnight before Christmas there was a great litter of fallen plastering, and laths, and chips, and shavings; and Elizabeth Eliza's carpet was taken up, and the furniture had to be changed, and one night she had to sleep at the Bromwiches', for there was a long hole in her floor that might be dangerous.

All this delighted the little boys. They could not understand what was going on. Perhaps they suspected a Christmas tree, but they did not know why a Christmas tree should have so many chips, and were still more astonished at the hump that appeared in Elizabeth Eliza's room. It must be a Christmas present, or else the tree in a box.

Some aunts and uncles, too, arrived a day or two before Christmas with some small cousins. These cousins occupied the attention of the little boys, and there was a great deal of whispering and mystery behind doors, and under the stairs, and in the corners of the entry.

Solomon John was busy, privately making some candles for the tree. He had been collecting some bayberries, as he understood they made very nice candles, so that it would not be necessary to buy any.

The elders of the family never all went into the back parlor together, and all tried not to see what was going on. Mrs. Peterkin would go in with Solomon John, or Mr. Peterkin would go with Elizabeth Eliza, or Elizabeth Eliza would go with Agamemnon and Solomon John. The little boys and the small cousins were never allowed even to look inside the room.

Elizabeth Eliza, meanwhile, went into town a number of times. She wanted to consult Amanda as to how much ice cream they should need, and whether they could make it at home, as they had cream and ice. She was pretty busy in her own room; the furniture had to be changed, and the carpet altered. The "hump" was higher than she had expected. There was danger of bumping her own head whenever she crossed it. She had to nail some padding on the ceiling for fear of accidents.

The afternoon before Christmas, Elizabeth Eliza, Solomon John, and their father collected in the back parlor for a council. The carpenters had done their work, and the tree stood at its full height at the back of the room, the top stretching up into the space arranged for it. All the chips and shavings were cleared away, and it stood on a neat box.

But what were they to put upon the tree?

Solomon John had brought in his supply of candles, but they proved to be very "stringy" and very few. It was strange how many bayberries it took to make a few candles! The little boys had helped him, and he had gathered as much as a bushel of bayberries. He had put them in water and skimmed off the wax, according to the directions, but there was so little wax!

After all her trips into town, Elizabeth Eliza had forgotten to bring anything for the tree.

"I thought of candies and sugarplums," she said, "but I concluded if we made caramels ourselves we should not need them. But, then, we have not made caramels. The fact is, that day my head was full of my carpet. I had bumped it pretty badly, too.

"It is odd I should have forgotten, that day I went in on purpose to get the things," said Elizabeth Eliza, musingly. "But I went from shop to shop and didn't know exactly what to get. I saw a great many gilt things for Christmas trees, but I knew the little boys were making the gilt apples; there were plenty of candles in the shops, but I knew Solomon John was making the candles."

Mr. Peterkin thought it was quite natural.

Solomon John wondered if it were too late for them to go into town now.

Elizabeth Eliza could not go the next morning, for there was to be a grand Christmas dinner, and Mr. Peterkin could not be spared, and Solomon John was sure he and Agamemnon would not know what to buy. Besides, they would want to try the candles tonight.

A gloom came over the room. There was only a flickering gleam from one of Solomon John's candles that he had lighted by way of trial.

Solomon John again proposed going into town. He lighted a match to read in the newspaper about the trains. There were plenty of trains coming out of town at that hour, but none going in except a very late one. That would not leave time to do anything and come back.

Agamemnon was summoned in. Mrs. Peterkin was entertaining the uncles and aunts in the front parlor. Agamemnon wished there were time to study up on electric lights. Solomon John's candle sputtered and went out.

At this moment there was a loud knocking at the front door. The little boys, and the small cousins, and the uncles and aunts, and Mrs. Peterkin hastened to see what was the matter.

The uncles and aunts thought somebody's house must be on fire. The door was opened and there was a man, white with flakes, for it was beginning to snow, and he was pulling in a large box.

Mrs. Peterkin supposed it contained some of Elizabeth Eliza's purchases, so she ordered it to be pushed into the back parlor, and hastily called back her guests and the boys into the other room. The little boys and the small cousins were sure they had seen Santa Claus himself.

Mr. Peterkin lighted the gas. The box was addressed to Elizabeth Eliza. It was from the lady from Philadelphia! She had gathered a hint from Elizabeth Eliza's letters that there was to be a Christmas tree, and she had filled this box with all that would be needed.

It was opened directly. There was every kind of gilt hanging thing, from gilt pods to butterflies on springs. There were shining flags and lanterns, and bird-cages, and nests with birds sitting on them, baskets of fruit, gilt apples, and bunches of grapes, and, at the bottom of the whole, a large box of candles and a box of Philadelphia bonbons!

Elizabeth Eliza and Solomon John could scarcely keep from screaming. The little boys and the small cousins knocked on the folding doors to ask what was the matter.

Hastily Mr. Peterkin and the rest took out the things and hung them on the tree and put on the candles.

When all was done, it looked so well that Mr. Peterkin exclaimed:

"Let us light the candles now, and send to invite all the neighbors tonight, and have the tree on Christmas Eve!"

And so it was that the Peterkins had their Christmas tree the day before, and on Christmas night could go and visit their neighbors.

Away in a Manger
Martin Luther
German Folk Melody
A - way in a man - ger, no crib for his bed, The
lit - tle Lord Je - sus lay down his sweet head; The
stars in the heav - ens Look'd down where he lay, The
lit - tle Lord Je - sus a - sleep on the hay.

The cattle are lowing,
The poor Baby wakes,
But little Lord Jesus
No crying He makes,

I love Thee Lord Jesus,
Look down from the sky,
And stay by my cradle
Till morning is nigh.

Be near me, Lord Jesus,
I ask Thee to stay
Close by me forever,
And love me I pray.

Bless all the dear children
In Thy tender care,
And take us to heaven,
To live with Thee there.

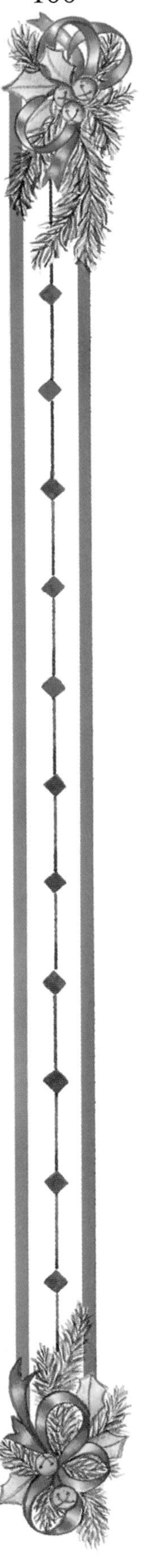

Susie's Letter from Santa

Mark Twain

My dear Susie Clemens:

I have received and read all the letters which you and your little sister have written me by the hand of your mother and your nurses; I have also read those which you little people have written me with your own hands—for although you did not use any characters that are in grown people's alphabet, you used the characters that all children in all lands on earth and in the twinkling stars use; and as all my subjects in the moon are children and use no characters but that, you will easily understand that I can read your and your baby sister's jagged and fantastic marks without any trouble at all. But I had trouble with those letters which you dictated through your mother and the nurses, for I am a foreigner and cannot read English writing well. You will find that I made no mistakes about the things which you and the baby ordered in your own letters—I went down your chimney at midnight when you were asleep and delivered them all myself and kissed both of you, too, because you are good children, well trained, nice mannered, and about the most obedient little people I ever saw. But in the letter which you dictated there were some words which I could not make out for certain, and one or two small orders which I could not fill because we ran out of stock. Our last lot of kitchen furniture for dolls has just gone to a very poor little child in the North away up in the cold country above the Big Dipper. Your mama can show you that star and you will say: "Little Snow Flake" (for that is the child's name), "I'm glad you got that furniture, for you need it more than I." That is, you must write that, with your own hand, and Snow Flake will write you an answer. If you only spoke it she wouldn't hear. Make your letter light and thin, for the distance is great and the postage very heavy.

There was a word or two in your mama's letter which I couldn't be certain of. I took it to be "a trunk full of doll's clothes." Is that it? I will call at your kitchen door about nine o'clock this morning to inquire. But I must not see anybody and I must not speak to anybody but you. When the kitchen doorbell rings, George must be blindfolded and sent to open the door. Then he must go back to the dining room or the china closet and take the cook with him. You must tell George he must walk on tiptoe and not speak—otherwise he will die someday. Then you must go up to the nursery and stand on a chair or the nurse's bed and put your ear to the speaking tube that leads down to the kitchen and when I whistle through it you must speak in the tube and say, "Welcome, Santa Claus!" Then I will ask whether it was a trunk you ordered or not. If you say it was, I shall ask you what color you want the trunk to be. Your mama will help you to name a nice color and then you must tell me every single thing in detail which you want the trunk to contain. Then when I say "Good-bye and a merry Christmas to my little Susie Clemens," you must say "Good-bye, good old Santa Claus, I thank you very much and please tell that little Snow Flake I will look at her star tonight and she must look down here. I will be right in the west bay window; and

every fine night I will look at her star and say, 'I know somebody up there and like her, too.' " Then you must go down into the library and make George close the doors that open into the main hall and everybody must keep still for a little while. Then while you are waiting I will go to the moon and get those things and in a few minutes I will come down the chimney that belongs to the fireplace that is in the hall—if it is a trunk you want—because I couldn't get such a large thing as a trunk down the nursery chimney, you know.

People may talk if they want, till they hear my footsteps in the hall. Then you tell them to keep quiet a little while until I get up the chimney. Maybe you will not hear my footsteps at all so you may go now and then and peep through the dining-room doors, and by and by you will see that which you want, right under the piano in the drawing room—for I shall put it there. If I should leave any snow in the hall, you must tell George to sweep it into the fireplace, for I haven't time to do such things. George must not use a broom, but a rag—or he will die someday. You watch George and don't let him run into danger. If my boot should leave a stain on the marble, George must not holystone it away. Leave it there always in memory of my visit; and whenever you look at it or show it to anybody you must let it remind you to be a good little girl. Whenever you are naughty and somebody points to that mark which your good old Santa Claus's boot made on the marble, what will you say, little sweetheart?

Good-bye for a few minutes, till I come down and ring the kitchen doorbell. Your loving Santa Claus whom people sometimes call "The Man in the Moon."

A Merry Christmas to You
Unknown Nineteenth- or Twentieth-Century Artist

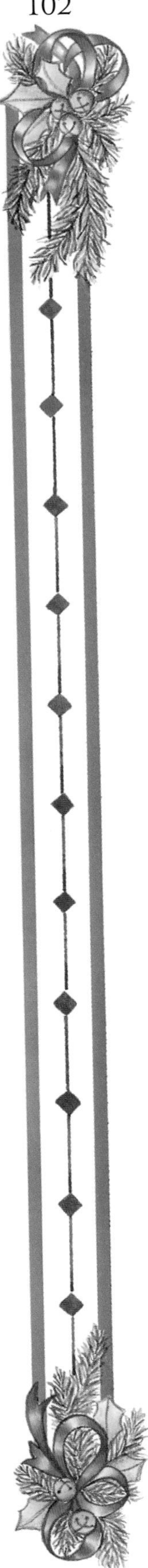

Annie and Willie's Prayer

Sophie P. Snow

'Twas the eve before Christmas; goodnight had been said,
And Annie and Willie had crept into bed.
'There were tears on their pillows and tears in their eyes,
And each little bosom was heaving with sighs;
For tonight their stern father's command had been given
That they should retire precisely at seven
Instead of at eight; for they troubled him more
With questions unheard of ever before.

He told them he thought this delusion a sin—
No such thing as Santa Claus ever had been.
And he hoped, after this, he would never more hear
How he scrambled down chimneys with presents each year.

And this was the reason that two little heads
So restlessly tossed on their soft, downy beds.
Eight, nine, and the clock in the steeple tolled ten;
Not a word had been spoken by either till then.
When Willie's sad face from the blanket did peep,
And whispered, "Dear Annie, is you fast asleep?"

"Why, no, brother Willie," a sweet voice replied,
"I've tried in vain, but I can't shut my eyes,
For somehow it makes me so sorry because
Dear Papa said there is no Santa Claus;
Now we know that there is, and it can't be denied,
For he came every year before Mamma died.
But then I am thinking that she used to pray,
And God would hear everything Mamma would say.
And perhaps she asked Him to send Santa Claus here
With the sacks full of presents he brought every year."

"Well, why tan't we pray dest as Mamma did then
And ask Him to send him presents aden?"
"I've been thinking so too." And without a word more,
Four little bare feet bounded out on the floor.
Four little knees the soft carpet pressed,
And two tiny hands were clasped close to each breast.
"Now, Willie, you know we must firmly believe
That the presents we ask for we're sure to receive;
You must wait just as still till I say the 'amen,'
And by that you will know that your turn has come then.

"Dear Jesus, look down on my brother and me,
And grant us the favor we are asking of Thee:
I want a wax dolly, a tea set and ring,
And an ebony workbox that locks with a spring.

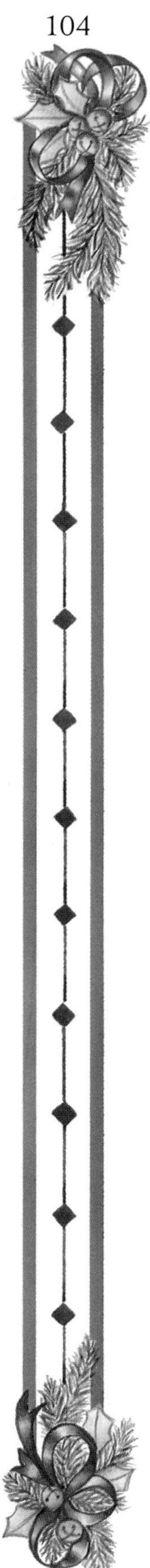

Bless Papa, dear Jesus, and cause him to see
That Santa Claus loves us far better than he.
Don't let him get fretful and angry again
At dear brother Willie and Annie. Amen."

"Please, Desus, let Santa Taus tum down tonight,
And bring us some presents before it is light.
I want he should div me a nice little sled
With b'ite shiny runners and all painted red;
A box full of tandy, a book and a toy,
Then Desus, I'll be a dood boy. Amen."

Their prayers being ended, they raised up their heads,
And with hearts light and cheerful again sought their bed.
They were soon lost in slumber, both peaceful and deep
And with fairies in dreamland were roaming in sleep.

Eight, nine, and the little French clock had struck ten,
Ere the father had thought of his children again;
He seems now to hear Annie's suppressed sighs,
And to see the big tears stand in Willie's blue eyes.

"I was harsh with my darlings," he mentally said,
"And should not have sent them so early to bed;
But then, I was troubled, my feelings found vent,
For bank stock today has gone down ten percent.

But of course they've forgotten their troubles ere this,
And that I denied them the thrice-asked-for kiss.
But just to be sure I'll steal up to their door,
For I never spoke harsh to my darlings before."
So saying, he softly ascended the stairs
And arrived at the door to hear both of their prayers.

His Annie's "Bless Papa" draws forth the big tears,
And Willie's grave promise falls sweet on his ears.
"Strange, strange, I'd forgotten," he said with a sigh,
"How I longed when a child to have Christmas draw nigh.
I'll atone for my harshness," he inwardly said,
"By answering their prayers ere I sleep in my bed."

Then he turned to the stairs, and softly went down,
Threw off velvet slippers and silk dressing gown,
Donned hat, coat, and boots, and was out in the street,
A millionaire facing the cold, driving sleet.

Nor stopped he until he had bought everything,
From a box full of candy to a tiny, gold ring.
Indeed, he kept adding so much to his store
That the various presents outnumbered a score.
Then homeward he turned with his holiday load,
And with Aunt Mary's aid in the nursery was stowed.

Miss dolly was seated beneath a pine tree,
By the side of a table spread out for a tea.
A workbox well-filled in the center was laid,
And on it the ring for which Annie had prayed.
A soldier in uniform stood by a sled,
With bright, shining runners, and all painted red.
There were balls, dogs, and horses, books pleasing to see
And birds of all colors were perched in the tree;
While Santa Claus, laughing, stood up on the top,

And as the fond father, the picture surveyed,
He thought for his trouble he had amply been paid;
And he said to himself, as he brushed off a tear,
I'm happier tonight than I've been for a year.
I've enjoyed more true pleasure than ever before,
What care I if bank stock falls ten percent more?
Hereafter I'll make it a rule, I believe,
To have Santa Claus visit us each Christmas Eve.
So thinking, he gently extinguished the light,
Then tripped down the stairs to retire for the night.

As soon as the beams of the bright morning sun
Put the darkness to flight, and the stars, one by one,
Four little blue eyes out of sleep opened wide,
And at the same moment the presents espied.
Then out of their bed they sprang with a bound,
And the very gifts prayed for were all of them found.
They laughed and they cried in their innocent glee
And shouted for Papa to come quick and see
What presents old Santa Claus brought in the night,
(Just the things that they wanted) and left before light.

"And now," added Annie, in a voice soft and low,
"You'll believe there's a Santa Claus, Papa, I know."
While dear little Willie climbed up on his knee,
Determined no secret between them should be.
And told in soft whispers how Annie had said
That their dear, blessed mamma so long ago dead
Used to kneel down and pray by the side of her chair,
And that God up in heaven had answered her prayer!
"Then we dot up and prayed dust as well as we tould,
And Dod answered our prayers; now wasn't He dood?"

"I should say that He was if He sent you all these,
And knew just what presents my children would please."
(Well, well, let him think so, the dear little elf;
Would be cruel to tell him I did it myself.)
Blind father! Who caused your proud heart to relent;
And the hasty words spoken so soon to repent?
'Twas Lord Jesus who bade you steal softly upstairs,
And made you His agent to answer their prayers.

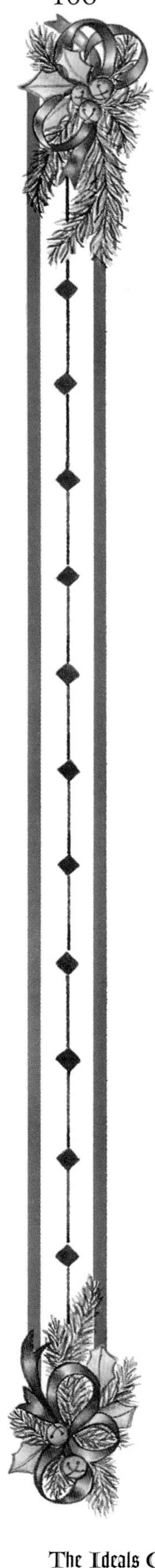

Greetings from Santa

Author Unknown

He comes in the night!
He comes in the night!
He softly, silently comes,
While the little brown heads on the pillows so white
Are dreaming of bugles and drums.
Who tells him, I know not,
But he finds the home
Of each good little boy and girl.

His sleigh, it is long and deep and wide;
It will carry a host of things,
While dozens of drums hang over the side,
With the sticks sticking under the strings.
And yet, not the sound of a drum is heard,
Not a bugle blast is blown,
As he mounts to the chimney top like a bird
And drops to the hearth like a stone.

The little red stockings, he silently fills
Till the stockings will hold no more;
The bright little sleds for the great snow hills
Are quickly set down on the floor.
Then Santa Claus mounts to the roof like a bird
And glides to his seat in the sleigh;
Not a sound of a bugle or drum is heard
As he noiselessly gallops away.

He rides to the East, and he rides to the West,
Of his goodies, he touches not one;
He eats the crumbs of the Christmas feast
When the dear little folks are done.
Old Santa Claus does all that he can;
This beautiful mission is his;
Then children, be good to the little old man,
When you find who the little man is.

Santa Fills the Stockings

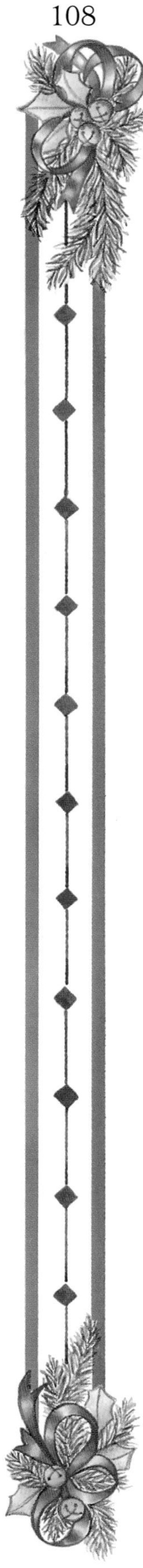

A Visit from St. Nicholas

Clement C. Moore

'Twas the night before Christmas, when all through the house
Not a creature was stirring, not even a mouse;
The stockings were hung by the chimney with care,
In hopes that St. Nicholas soon would be there.
The children were nestled all snug in their beds,
While visions of sugarplums danced through their heads;
And Mamma in her kerchief, and I in my cap,
Had just settled our brains for a long winter's nap—
When out on the lawn there arose such a clatter,
I sprang from my bed to see what was the matter.
Away to the window I flew like a flash,
Tore open the shutters and threw up the sash.
The moon on the breast of the new-fallen snow
Gave the luster of midday to objects below;
When, what to my wondering eyes should appear,
But a miniature sleigh and eight tiny reindeer,
With a little old driver, so lively and quick,
I knew in a moment it must be St. Nick.
More rapid than eagles his coursers they came
And he whistled, and shouted, and called them by name:
"Now, Dasher! now, Dancer! now, Prancer! and Vixen!
On, Comet! on, Cupid! on, Donder and Blitzen!
To the top of the porch! to the top of the wall!
Now dash away! dash away! dash away all!"
As dry leaves that before the wild hurricane fly,
When they meet with an obstacle, mount to the sky,
So up to the housetop the coursers they flew,
With the sleighful of toys, and St. Nicholas too.
And then in a twinkling I heard on the roof
The prancing and pawing of each little hoof.
As I drew in my head, and was turning around,
Down the chimney St. Nicholas came with a bound.
He was dressed all in fur from his head to his foot,
And his clothes were all tarnished with ashes and soot;
A bundle of toys he had flung on his back,
And he looked like a peddler just opening his pack.
His eyes, how they twinkled! his dimples, how merry!
His cheeks were like roses, his nose like a cherry!
His droll little mouth was drawn up like a bow,
And the beard on his chin was as white as the snow.

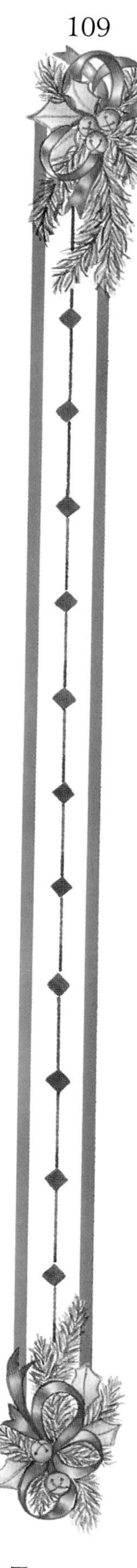

The stump of a pipe he held tight in his teeth,
And the smoke, it encircled his head like a wreath.
He had a broad face, and a little round belly
That shook, when he laughed, like a bowl full of jelly.
He was chubby and plump—a right jolly old elf;
And I laughed, when I saw him, in spite of myself.
A wink of his eye, and a twist of his head
Soon gave me to know I had nothing to dread.
He spoke not a word, but went straight to his work,
And filled all the stockings; then turned with a jerk,
And laying his finger aside of his nose,
And giving a nod, up the chimney he rose.
He sprang to his sleigh, to the team gave a whistle,
And away they all flew, like the down of a thistle,
But I heard him exclaim, ere he drove out of sight,
"Happy Christmas to all, and to all a good-night!"

Delivering Presents
Unknown Nineteenth-Century Artist

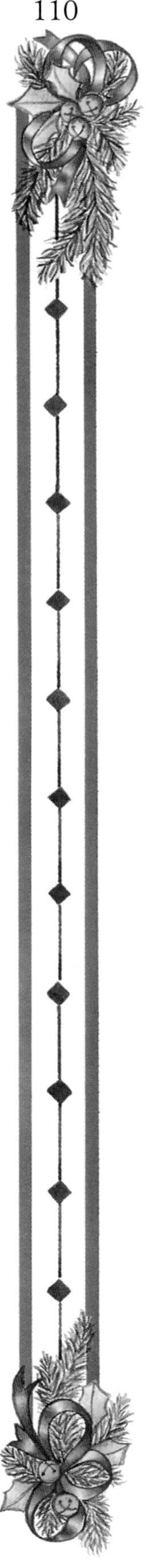

Little Jesus, Wast Thou Shy?

Francis Thompson

Little Jesus, wast Thou shy
Once, and just so small as I
And what did it feel like to be
Out of Heaven, and just like me?
Didst Thou sometimes think of there,
And ask where all the angels were?

I should think that I would cry
For my house all made of sky;
I would look about the air,
And wonder where my angels were;
And at waking 'twould distress me—
Not an angel there to dress me!

Hadst Thou ever any toys,
Like us little girls and boys?
And didst Thou play in heaven with all
The angels that were not too tall,
With stars for marbles? Did the things
Play "Can you see me?" through their wings?

Didst Thou kneel at night to pray,
And didst Thou join Thy hands, this way?
And didst Thy tire sometimes, being young,
And make the prayer seem very long?
And dost Thou like it best, that we
Should join our hands to pray to Thee?

I used to think, before I knew,
The prayer not said unless we do.
And did Thy Mother at the night
Kiss Thee, and fold Thy clothes in right?
And didst Thou feel quite good in bed,
Kissed, and sweet, and Thy prayers said?

Thou canst not have forgotten all
That it feels like to be small.
And Thou know'st I cannot pray
To Thee in my father's way—
When Thou wast so little, say,

Couldst Thou talk Thy Father's way?
So, a little Child, come down
And hear a child's tongue like Thy own;
Take me by the hand and walk,
And listen to my baby talk.
To Thy Father show my prayer
(He will look, Thou art so fair),
And say: "O Father, I, Thy Son,
Bring the prayer of a little one."

And He will smile, that children's tongue
Has not changed since Thou wast young!

Little Girl and Toys Kneeling by Bedside, c. 1900

Christmas Is for Giving

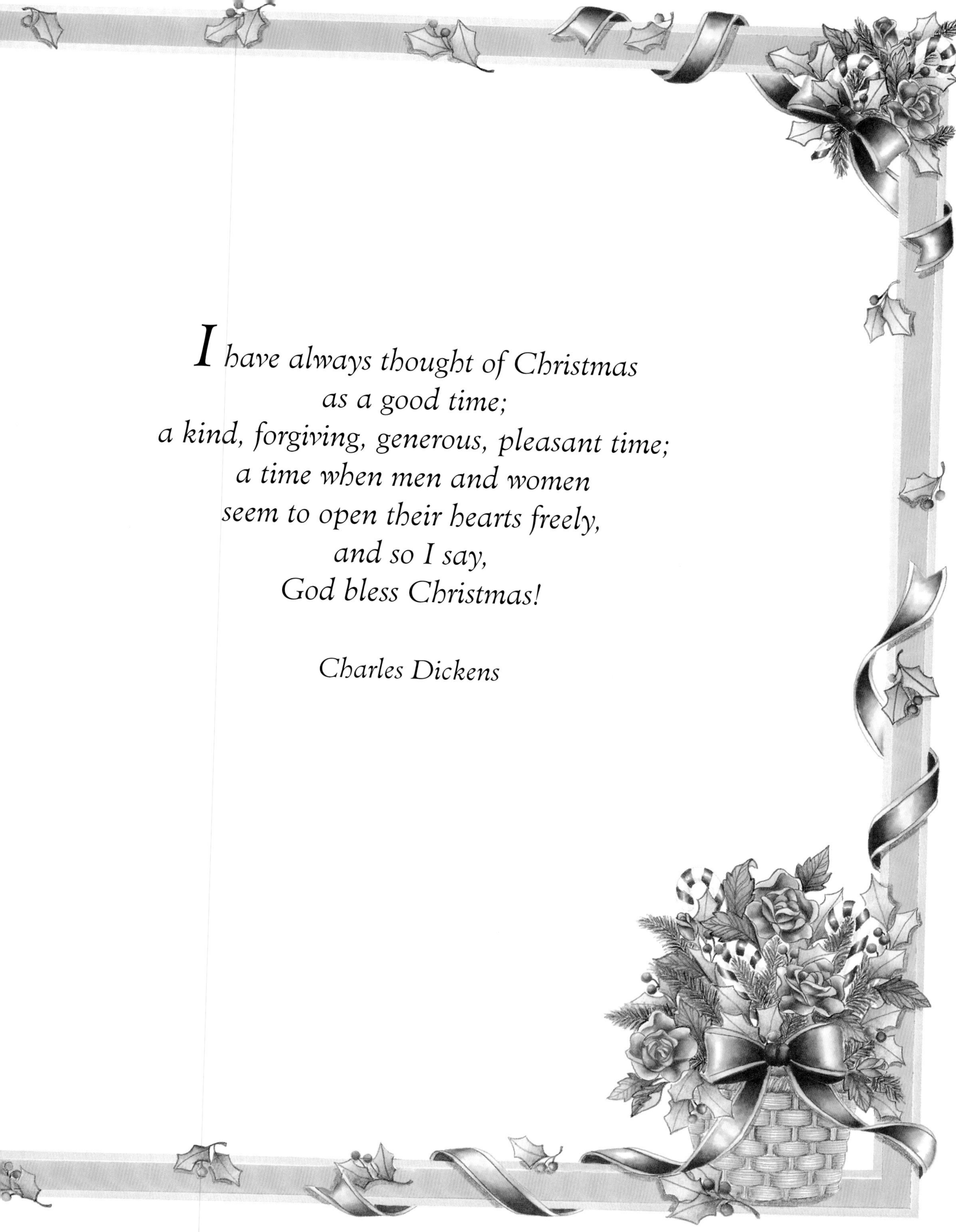

I have always thought of Christmas
as a good time;
a kind, forgiving, generous, pleasant time;
a time when men and women
seem to open their hearts freely,
and so I say,
God bless Christmas!

Charles Dickens

A Gift of the Heart

Norman Vincent Peale

New York City, where I live, is impressive at any time, but as Christmas approaches it's overwhelming. Store windows blaze with lights and color, furs and jewels. Golden angels, forty feet tall, hover over Fifth Avenue. Wealth, power, opulence . . . nothing in the world can match this fabulous display.

Through the gleaming canyons, people hurry to find last-minute gifts. Money seems to be no problem. If there's a problem, it's that the recipients so often have everything they need or want that it's hard to find anything suitable, anything that will really say, "I love you."

Last December, as Christ's birthday drew near, a stranger was faced with just that problem. She had come from Switzerland to live in an American home and perfect her English. In return, she was willing to act as secretary, mind the grandchildren, do anything she was asked. Her name was Ursula.

One of the tasks her employers gave Ursula was keeping track of Christmas presents as they arrived. There were many, and all would require acknowledgment. Ursula kept a faithful record, but with a growing sense of concern. She was grateful to her American friends; she wanted to show her gratitude by giving them a Christmas present. But nothing that she could buy with her small allowance could compare with the gifts she was recording daily. Besides, even without these gifts, it seemed to her that her employers already had everything.

At night from her window Ursula could see the snowy expanse of Central Park and beyond it the jagged skyline of the city. Far below, taxis hooted and the traffic lights winked red and green. It was so different from the silent majesty of the Alps that at times she had to blink back tears of the homesickness she was careful never to show. It was in the solitude of her little room, a few days before Christmas, that her secret idea came to Ursula.

It was almost as if a voice spoke clearly, inside her head. "It's true," said the voice, "that many people in this city have much more than you do. But surely there are many who have far less. If you will think about this, you may find a solution to what's troubling you."

Ursula thought long and hard. Finally on her day off, which was Christmas Eve, she went to a large department store. She moved slowly along the crowded aisles, selecting and rejecting things in her mind. At last she bought something and had it wrapped in gaily colored paper. She went out into the gray twilight and looked helplessly around. Finally, she went up to a doorman, resplendent in blue and gold. "Excuse, please," she said in her hesitant English, "can you tell me where to find a poor street?"

"A poor street, Miss?" said the puzzled man.

"Yes, a very poor street. The poorest in the city."

The doorman looked doubtful. "Well, you might try Harlem. Or down in the

Village. Or the Lower East Side, maybe."

But these names meant nothing to Ursula. She thanked the doorman and walked along, threading her way through the stream of shoppers until she came to a tall policeman. "Please," she said, "can you direct me to a very poor street in . . . in Harlem?"

The policeman looked at her sharply and shook his head. "Harlem's no place for you, Miss." And he blew his whistle and sent the traffic swirling past.

Holding her package carefully, Ursula walked on, head bowed against the sharp wind. If a street looked poorer than the one she was on, she took it. But none seemed like the slums she had heard about. Once she stopped a woman, "Please, where do the very poor people live?" But the woman gave her a stare and hurried on.

Darkness came sifting from the sky. Ursula was cold and discouraged and afraid of becoming lost. She came to an intersection and stood forlornly on the corner. What she was trying to do suddenly seemed foolish, impulsive, absurd. Then through the traffic's roar, she heard the cheerful tinkle of a bell. On the corner opposite, a Salvation Army man was making his traditional

With Father Christmas's Love
Unknown Nineteenth-Century Artist

Christmas appeal.

At once Ursula felt better; the Salvation Army was a part of life in Switzerland too. Surely this man could tell her what she wanted to know. She waited for the light, then crossed over to him. "Can you help me? I'm looking for a baby. I have here a little present for the poorest baby I can find." And she held up the package with the green ribbon and the gaily colored paper.

Dressed in gloves and overcoat a size too big for him, he seemed a very ordinary man. But behind his steel-rimmed glasses his eyes were kind. He looked at Ursula and stopped ringing his bell. "What sort of present?" he asked.

"A little dress. For a small, poor baby. Do you know of one?"

"Oh, yes," he said. "Of more than one, I'm afraid."

"Is it far away? I could take a taxi, maybe?"

The Salvation Army man wrinkled his forehead. Finally he said, "It's almost six o'clock. My relief will show up then. If you want to wait, and if you can afford a dollar taxi ride, I'll take you to a family in my own neighborhood who needs just about everything."

"And they have a small baby?"

"A very small baby."

"Then," said Ursula joyfully, "I wait!"

The substitute bell-ringer came. A cruising taxi slowed. In its welcome warmth, Ursula told her new friend about herself, how she came to be in New York, what she was trying to do. He listened in silence, and the taxi driver listened too. When they reached their destination, the driver said, "Take your time, Miss. I'll wait for you."

On the sidewalk, Ursula stared up at the forbidding tenement, dark, decaying, saturated with hopelessness. A gust of wind, iron-cold, stirred the refuse in the street and rattled the ashcans. "They live on the third floor," the Salvation Army man said. "Shall we go up?"

But Ursula shook her head. "They would try to thank me, and this is not from me." She pressed the package into his hand. "Take it up for me, please. Say it's from . . . from someone who has everything."

The taxi bore her swiftly back from dark streets to lighted ones, from misery to abundance. She tried to visualize the Salvation Army man climbing the stairs, the knock, the explanation, the package being opened, the dress on the baby. It was hard to do.

Arriving at the apartment house on Fifth Avenue where she lived, she fumbled in her purse. But the driver flicked the flag up. "No charge, Miss."

"No charge?" echoed Ursula, bewildered.

"Don't worry," the driver said. "I've been paid." He smiled at her and drove away.

Ursula was up early the next day. She set the table with special care. By the time she had finished, the family was awake, and there was all the excitement and laughter of Christmas morning. Soon the living room was a sea of gay discarded wrappings. Ursula thanked everyone for the presents she received. Finally, when there was a lull, she began to explain hesitantly why there seemed to be none from her. She told about going to the department store. She told about the Salvation Army man. She told about the taxi driver. When she finished, there was a long silence. No one seemed to trust himself to speak. "So you see," said Ursula, "I try to do a kindness in your name. And this is my Christmas present to you. . . ."

How do I happen to know all this? I know because ours was the home where Ursula lived. Ours was the Christmas she shared. We were like many Americans, so richly blessed that to this child from across the sea there seemed to be nothing she could add to the material things we already had. And so she offered something of far greater value: a gift of the heart, an act of kindness carried out in our name.

Strange, isn't it? A shy Swiss girl, alone in a great impersonal city. You would think that nothing she could do would affect anyone. And yet, by trying to give away love, she brought the true spirit of Christmas into our lives, the spirit of selfless giving. That was Ursula's secret—and she shared it with us all.

Christmas Greetings!
Anonymous, Twentieth Century

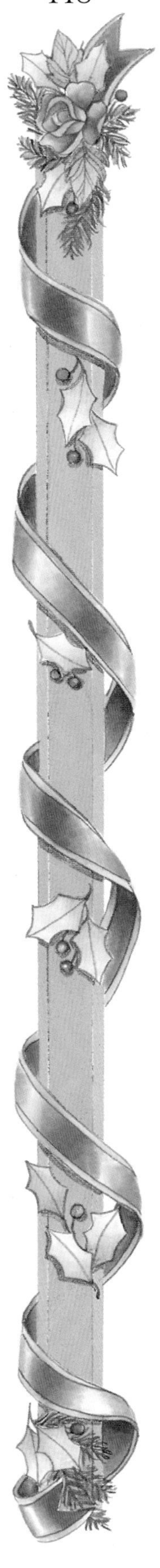

Christmas Trees

Robert Frost

The city had withdrawn into itself
And left at last the country to the country;
When between whirls of snow not come to lie
And whirls of foliage not yet laid, there drove
A stranger to our yard, who looked the city,
Yet did in country fashion in that there
He sat and waited till he drew us out
A-buttoning coats to ask him who he was.
He proved to be the city come again
To look for something it had left behind
And could not do without and keep its Christmas.
He asked if I would sell my Christmas trees;
My woods—the young fir balsams like a place
Where houses all are churches and have spires.
I hadn't thought of them as Christmas trees.
I doubt if I was tempted for a moment
To sell them off their feet to go in cars
And leave the slope behind the house all bare,
Where the sun shines now no warmer than the moon.
I'd hate to have them know it if I was.
Yet more I'd hate to hold my trees except
As others hold theirs or refuse for them,
Beyond the time of profitable growth,
The trial by market everything must come to.
I dallied so much with the thought of selling.
Then whether from mistaken courtesy
And fear of seeming short of speech, or whether
From hope of hearing good of what was mine,
I said, "There aren't enough to be worth while."

"I could soon tell how many they would cut,
You let me look them over."

"You could look.
But don't expect I'm going to let you have them."
Pasture they spring in, some in clumps too close
That lop each other of boughs, but not a few
Quite solitary and having equal boughs
All round and round. The latter he nodded "Yes" to,
Or paused to say beneath some lovelier one,
With a buyer's moderation, "That would do."
I thought so too, but wasn't there to say so.
We climbed the pasture on the south, crossed over,
And came down on the north.
He said, "A thousand."
A thousand trees would come to thirty dollars."

Then I was certain I had never meant
To let him have them. Never show surprise!
But thirty dollars seemed so small beside
The extent of pasture I should strip, three cents
(For that was all they figured out apiece),
Three cents so small beside the dollar friends
I should be writing to within the hour
Would pay in cities for good trees like those,
Regular vestry-trees whole Sunday Schools
Could hang enough on to pick off enough.
A thousand Christmas trees I didn't know I had!
Worth three cents more to give away than sell
As may be shown by a simple calculation.
Too bad I couldn't lay one in a letter.
I can't help wishing I could send you one,
In wishing you herewith a Merry Christmas.

Girl in Sleigh, Boy with Lantern
Uknown Twentieth-Century Artist

All the Days of Christmas

Phyllis McGinley

What shall my true love
Have from me
To pleasure his Christmas
Wealthily?
The partridge has flown
From our pear tree.
Flown with our summers
Are the swans and the geese.
Milkmaids and drummers
Would leave him little peace.
I've no gold ring
And no turtle dove,
So what can I bring
To my true love?

A coat for the drizzle
Chosen at the store;
A saw and a chisel
For mending the door;
A pair of red slippers
To slip on his feet;
Three striped neckties;
Something sweet.

He shall have all
I can best afford—
No pipers piping,
No leaping Lord,
But a fine fat hen
For his Christmas board;
Two pretty daughters
(Versed in the role)
To be worn like pinks
In his buttonhole
And the tree of my heart
With its calling linnet—
My evergreen heart
And the bright bird in it.

Christmas Eve
Walter Anderson

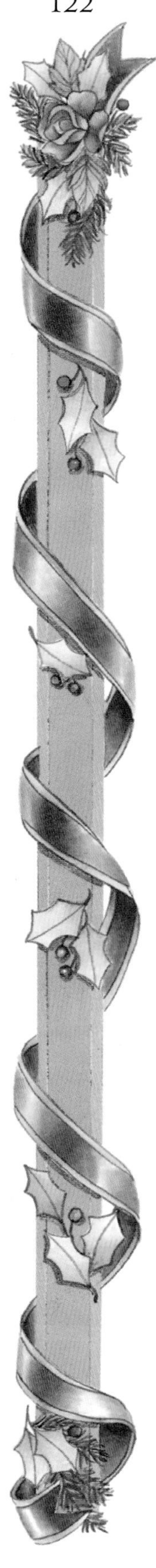

The Legend of the Christmas Tree

Clement Clarke Moore

Most children have seen a Christmas tree, and many know that the pretty and pleasant custom of hanging gifts on its boughs comes from Germany; but perhaps few have heard or read the story that is told to little German children, respecting the origin of this custom. The story is called "The Little Stranger," and runs thus:

In a small cottage on the borders of a forest lived a poor laborer, who gained a scanty living by cutting wood. He had a wife and two children who helped him in his work. The boy's name was Valentine, and the girl was called Mary. They were obedient, good children, and a great comfort to their parents. One winter evening, this happy little family were sitting quietly round the hearth, the snow and the wind raging outside, while they ate their supper of dry bread, when a gentle tap was heard on the window, and a childish voice cried from without; "Oh, let me in, pray! I am a poor child, with nothing to eat, and no home to go to, and I shall die of cold and hunger unless you let me in."

Valentine and Mary jumped up from the table and ran to open the door, saying: "Come in, poor little child! We have not much to give you, but whatever we have we will share with you."

The stranger-child came in and warmed his frozen hands and feet at the fire, and the children gave him the best they had to eat, saying: "You must be tired, too, poor child! Lie down on our bed; we can sleep on the bench for one night."

Then said the little stranger-child: "Thank God for all your kindness to me!"

So they took their little guest into their sleeping-room, laid him on the bed, covered him over, and said to each other: "How thankful we ought to be! We have warm rooms and a cozy bed, while this poor child has only heaven for his roof and the cold earth for his sleeping-place."

When their father and mother went to bed, Mary and Valentine lay quite contentedly on the bench near the fire, saying, before they fell asleep: "The stranger-child will be so happy tonight in his warm bed!"

These kind children had not slept many hours before Mary awoke, and softly whispered to her brother: "Valentine, dear, wake, and listen to the sweet music under the window."

Then Valentine rubbed his eyes and listened. It was sweet music indeed, and sounded like beautiful voices singing to the tones of a harp:

Oh holy Child, we greet thee! bringing
Sweet strains of harp to aid our singing.
Thou, holy Child, in peace art sleeping,
While we our watch without are keeping.
Blest be the house wherein Thou liest,
Happiest on earth, to heaven the Highest.

The children listened, while a solemn joy filled their hearts; then they stepped softly to the window to see who might be without.

In the east was a streak of rosy dawn, and in its light they saw a group of chil-

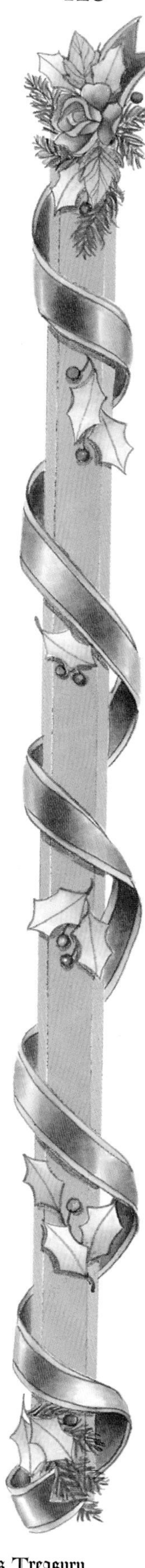

dren standing before the house, clothed in silver garments, holding golden harps in their hands. Amazed at this sight, the children were still gazing out of the window, when a light tap caused them to turn around. There stood the stranger-child before them clad in a golden dress, with a gleaming radiance round his curling hair. "I am the little Christ child," he said, "who wanders through the world bringing peace and happiness to good children. You took me in and cared for me when you thought me a poor child, and now you shall have my blessing for what you have done."

A fir tree grew near the house; and from this he broke a twig, which he planted in the ground, saying: "This twig shall become a tree, and shall bring forth fruit year by year for you."

No sooner had he done this than he vanished, and with him the little choir of angels. But the fir branch grew and became a Christmas tree, and on its branches hung golden apples and silver nuts every Christmastide.

Such is the story told to German children concerning their beautiful Christmas trees, though we know that the real little Christ child can never be wandering, cold and homeless, again in our world, inasmuch as He is safe in heaven by His Father's side; yet we may gather from this story the same truth which the Bible plainly tells us—that anyone who helps a child in distress, it will be counted unto him as if he had indeed done it unto Christ himself. "Inasmuch as ye have done it unto the least of these, my brethren, ye have done it unto me."

Christmas Living Room

Wise Men from the East

Matthew 2:1-13

Now when Jesus was born in Bethlehem of Judea in the days of Herod the king, behold, there came wise men from the east to Jerusalem, Saying, Where is he that is born King of the Jews? for we have seen his star in the east, and are come to worship him.

When Herod the king had heard these things, he was troubled, and all Jerusalem with him. And when he had gathered all the chief priests and scribes of the people together, he demanded of them where Christ should be born. And they said unto him, In Bethlehem of Judea: for thus it is written by the prophet, And thou Bethlehem, in the land of Juda, art not the least among the princes of Juda: for out of thee shall come a Governor, that shall rule my people Israel.

Then Herod, when he had privily called the wise men, enquired of them diligently what time the star appeared. And he sent them to Bethlehem, and said, Go and search diligently for the young child: and when ye have found him, bring me word again, that I may come and worship him also.

When they had heard the king, they departed; and lo, the star, which they saw in the east, went before them, till it came and stood over where the young child was. When they saw the star, they rejoiced with exceeding great joy.

And when they were come into the house, they saw the young child with Mary his mother, and fell down, and worshipped him: and when they had opened their treasures, they presented unto him gifts; gold, and frankincense, and myrrh. And being warned of God in a dream that they should not return to Herod, they departed into their own country another way.

We Three Kings of Orient Are

John H. Hopkins

Kings:
We three kings of Orient are;
Bearing gifts, we traverse afar
Field and fountain, moor and mountain,
Following yonder star.

O—Star of wonder, Star of night
Star with royal beauty bright,
Westward leading, still proceeding,
Guide us to the perfect light.

Melchior:
Born a King on Bethlehem's plain,
Gold I bring, to crown Him again,
King forever ceasing never
Over us all to reign.

O—Star of wonder, Star of night
Star with royal beauty bright,
Westward leading, still proceeding,
Guide us to the perfect light.

Casper:
Frankincense to offer have I,
Incense owns a Deity nigh.
Prayer and praising all men raising,
Worship Him, God most high.

O—Star of wonder, Star of night
Star with royal beauty bright,
Westward leading, still proceeding,
Guide us to the perfect light.

Balthazar:
Myrrh is mine, its bitter perfume
Breathes a life of gathering gloom;
Sorrowing, sighing, bleeding, dying,
Sealed in a stone-cold tomb.

O—Star of wonder, Star of night
Star with royal beauty bright,
Westward leading, still proceeding,
Guide us to the perfect light.

All:
Glorious now behold Him arise,
King and God and Sacrifice,
Alleluia, Alleluia,
Earth to the heavens replies.

O—Star of wonder, Star of night
Star with royal beauty bright,
Westward leading, still proceeding,
Guide us to the perfect light.

Our Lady's Juggler

Anatole France

In the days when the world was young, there lived in France a man of no importance. Everyone said he was a man of no importance, and he firmly believed this himself. For he was just a poor traveling juggler, who could not read or write, who went about from town to town following the little country fairs and performing his tricks for a few pennies a day. His name was Barnaby.

When the weather was beautiful, and people were strolling about the streets, this juggler would find a clear space in the Village Square, spread a strip of old carpet out on the cobblestones, and on it he would perform his tricks for children and grown-ups alike. Now Barnaby, although he knew he was a man of no importance, was an amazing juggler.

First he would only balance a tin plate on the tip of his nose. But when the crowd had collected, he would stand on his hands and juggle six copper balls in the air at the same time, catching them with his feet. And sometimes, when he would juggle twelve sharp knives in the air, the villagers would be so delighted that a rain of pennies would fall on his strip of carpet. And when his day's work was over, and he was wearily resting his aching muscles, Barnaby would collect the pennies in his hat, kneel down reverently, and thank God for the gift.

Always the people would laugh at his simplicity and everyone would agree that Barnaby would never amount to anything. But all this is about the happy days in Barnaby's life, the springtime days when people were willing to toss a penny to a poor juggler. When winter came, Barnaby had to wrap his juggling equipment in the carpet, and trudge along the roads begging a night's lodging in farmers' barns, or entertaining the servants of some rich nobleman to earn a meal. And Barnaby never thought of complaining—he knew that the winter and the rains were as necessary as the spring sunshine, and he accepted his lot. "For how," Barnaby would say to himself as he trudged along, "could such an ignorant fellow as myself hope for anything better."

And one year in France there was a terrible winter. It began to rain in October, and there was hardly a blue sky to be seen by the end of November. And on an evening in early December at the end of a dreary, wet day, as Barnaby trudged along a country road, sad and bent, carrying under his arm the golden balls and knives wrapped up in his old carpet, he met a monk. Riding a fine white mule, dressed in warm clothes, well fed and comfortable, the monk smiled at the sight of Barnaby and called to him:

Christmas Angels
Anonymous, Nineteenth Century

"It's going to be cold before morning. How would you like to spend the night at the monastery?"

And that night Barnaby found himself seated in the great candlelit dining hall of the monastery. Although he sat at the bottom of the long table, together with the servants and beggars, Barnaby thought he had never seen such a wonderful sight in his life—the shining faces of fifty monks relaxing after this day of work and prayer.

Barnaby did not dare to suggest that he should perform his tricks, as they would be sacrilege before such men; but as he ate and drank more than he had ever had at a meal for years, a great resolution came over him. Although it made him tremble at his own boldness, as the meal ended, Barnaby suddenly arose, ran around the table down to where the lordly abbot sat at the head, and sank to his knees. "Father, grant my prayer! Let me stay in this wonderful place and work for you! I cannot hope to become one of you, I am too ignorant; but let me work in the kitchen and the fields and worship with you in the chapel!"

The monk who had met Barnaby on the road turned to the abbot: "This is a good man, simple and pure of heart." So the abbot nodded, and Barnaby that night put his juggling equipment under a cot in his own cubicle, and decided that never again would he go back to his old profession.

And in the days that followed, everyone smiled at the eager way he scrubbed the floors and labored throughout the buildings; and everyone smiled at his simplicity. As for Barnaby, his face shone with happiness from morning until night.

Until two weeks before Christmas—then Barnaby's joy suddenly turned to misery. For around him he saw every man preparing a wonderful gift to place in the chapel on Christmas—Brother Maurice, who had the art of illuminating copies of the Bible, and Brother Marbode, who was completing a marvelous statue of Christ. Brother Ambrose, who wrote music, had completed the scoring of a great hymn to be played on the organ during Christmas services.

All about Barnaby those educated, trained artists followed their work, each one of them readying a beautiful gift to dedicate to God on Christmas Day. And what about Barnaby? He could do nothing. "I am but a rough man, unskilled in the arts, and I can write no book, offer no painting or statue or poem. Alas, I have no talent, I have no gift worthy of the day!"

So Barnaby sank deep into sadness and despair. Christmas Day came, and the chapel was resplendent with the gifts of the brothers. The giant organ rang with the new music; the choir sang the chorales; the candles glittered around the great new statue. And Barnaby was not there. He was in his tiny cubicle, praying for forgiveness for having no gift to offer.

Then a strange thing happened. On the evening of Christmas Day, when the chapel should have been deserted, one of the monks came running, white-faced and panting with exertion, into the private office of the abbot. He threw open the door without knocking, and seized the abbot by the arms. "Father, a frightful thing is happening. The most terrible sacrilege ever to take place is going on right in our own chapel! Come!"

Together the two portly men ran down the corridors, burst through a door, and came out on the balcony at the rear of the chapel. The monk pointed down toward the altar. The abbot looked and turned ashen in color. "He is mad!"

For down below, in front of the altar was Barnaby. He had spread out his strip of carpet and, kneeling reverently upon it, was actually juggling in the air twelve golden balls! He was giving his old performance, and giving it beautifully—his bright knives, the shining balls, the tin plate balanced on the tip of his nose. And on his face was a look of adoration and joy.

"We must seize him at once," cried the abbot and turned for the door. But at that moment a light filled the church, a brilliant beam of light coming directly from the altar. Both monks sank to their knees.

For as Barnaby knelt exhausted on his carpet, they saw the statue of the Virgin Mary move. She stepped down from her pedestal, and coming to where Barnaby knelt, took the blue hem of her robe and touched it to his forehead, gently drying the perspiration that glistened there. Then the light dimmed. Up in the choir balcony the monk looked at his superior: "God accepted the only gift he had to make."

And the abbot slowly nodded: "Blessed are the simple in heart . . . for they shall see God."

"And he opened his mouth,
and taught them, saying,
Blessed are the poor in spirit:
for theirs is the kingdom of heaven. . . .
Blessed are the pure in heart:
for they shall see God."

Matthew 5:2, 3, 8

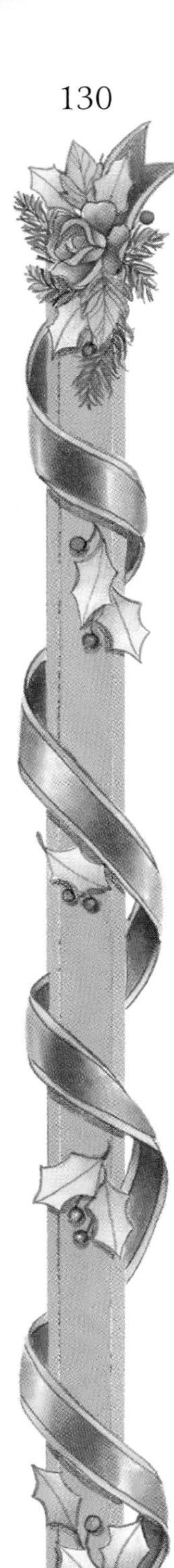

The Gift of the Magi

O. Henry

One dollar and eighty-seven cents. That was all. And sixty cents of it was in pennies. Pennies saved one and two at a time by bulldozing the grocer and the vegetable man and the butcher until one's cheeks burned with the silent imputation of parsimony that such close dealing implied. Three times Della counted it. One dollar and eighty-seven cents. And the next day would be Christmas.

There was clearly nothing to do but flop down on the shabby little couch and howl. So Della did it. Which instigates the moral reflection that life is made up of sobs, sniffles, and smiles, with sniffles predominating.

While the mistress of the home is gradually subsiding from the first stage to the second take a look at the home. A furnished flat at eight dollars per week. It did not exactly beggar description, but it certainly had that word on the lookout for the mendicancy squad.

In the vestibule below belonged to this flat a letter-box into which no letter would go, and an electric button from which no mortal finger could coax a ring. Also appertaining thereunto was a card bearing the name "Mr. James Dillingham Young."

The "Dillingham" had been flung to the breeze during a former period of prosperity when its possessor was being paid thirty dollars per week. Now, when the income was shrunk to $20, the letters of "Dillingham" looked blurred, as though they were thinking seriously of contracting to a modest and unassuming D. But whenever Mr. James Dillingham Young came home and reached his flat above he was called "Jim" and greatly hugged by Mrs. James Dillingham Young, already introduced to you as Della. Which is all very good.

Della finished her cry and attended to her cheeks with the powder rag. She stood by the window and looked out dully at a gray cat walking a gray fence in a gray backyard. Tomorrow would be Christmas Day, and she had only one dollar and eighty-seven cents with which to buy Jim a present. She had been saving every penny she could for months, with this result. Twenty dollars a week doesn't go far. Expenses had been greater than she had calculated. They always are. Only one dollar and eighty-seven cents to buy a present for Jim. Her Jim. Many a happy hour she had spent planning for something nice for him. Something fine and rare and sterling—something just a little bit near to being worthy of the honor of being owned by Jim.

There was a pier-glass between the windows of the room. Perhaps you have seen a pier-glass in an eight dollar flat. A very thin and very agile person may, by observing his reflection in a rapid sequence of longitudinal strips, obtain a fairly accurate conception of his looks. Della, being slender, had mastered the art.

Suddenly she whirled from the window and stood before the glass. Her eyes were shining brilliantly, but her face had lost its color within twenty seconds. Rapidly she pulled down her hair and let it fall to its full length.

Now, there were two possessions of the James Dillingham Youngs in which they both took a mighty pride. One was Jim's gold watch that had been his father's and his grandfather's. The other was Della's hair. Had the Queen of Sheba lived in the flat across the airshaft Della would have let her hair hang out the window some day to dry and mocked at Her Majesty's jewels and gifts. Had King Solomon been the janitor, with all his treasures piled up in the basement, Jim would have pulled out his watch every time he passed, just to see him pluck at his beard from envy.

So now Della's beautiful hair fell about her, rippling and shining like a cascade of brown waters. It reached below her knees and made itself almost a garment for her. And then she did it up again nervously and quickly. Once she faltered for a minute and stood still while a tear or two splashed on the worn red carpet.

On went her old brown jacket; on went her old brown hat. With a whirl of skirts and with the brilliant sparkle still in her eyes, she fluttered out the door and down the stairs to the street.

Where she stopped the sign read: "Mme. Sofronie. Hair Goods of All Kinds." One flight up Della ran, and collected herself, panting, before madame, large, too white, chilly and hardly looking the "Sofronie."

"Will you buy my hair?" asked Della.

"I buy hair," said Madame. "Take yer hat off and let's have a sight at the looks of it."

Down rippled the brown cascade.

"Twenty dollars," said Madame, lifting the mass with a practiced hand.

"Give it to me quick," said Della.

Oh, and the next two hours tripped by on rosy wings. Forget the hashed metaphor. She was ransacking the stores for Jim's present.

Antique Christmas Card

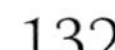

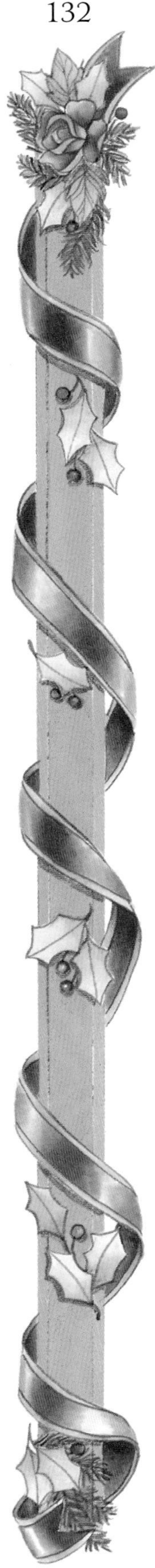

She found it at last. It surely had been made for Jim and no one else. There was none other like it in any of the stores, and she had turned all of them inside out. It was a platinum fob chain simple and chaste in design, properly proclaiming its value by substance alone and not by meretricious ornamentation—as all good things should do. It was even worthy of The Watch. As soon as she saw it she knew that it must be Jim's. It was like him. Quietness and value—the description applied to both. Twenty-one dollars they took from her for it, and she hurried home with the eighty-seven cents. With that chain on his watch Jim might be properly anxious about the time in any company. Grand as the watch was, he sometimes looked at it on the sly on account of the old leather strap that he used in place of a chain.

When Della reached home her intoxication gave way a little to prudence and reason. She got out her curling irons and lighted the gas and went to work repairing the ravages made by generosity added to love. Which is always a tremendous task, dear friends—a mammoth task.

Within forty minutes her head was covered with tiny, close-lying curls that made her look wonderfully like a truant schoolboy. She looked at her reflection in the mirror long, carefully, and critically.

"If Jim doesn't kill me," she said to herself, "before he takes a second look at me, he'll say I look like a Coney Island chorus girl. But what could I do—oh, what could I do with a dollar and eighty-seven cents!"

At seven o'clock the coffee was made and the frying pan was on the back of the stove hot and ready to cook the chops.

Jim was never late. Della doubled the fob chain in her hand and sat on the corner of the table near the door that he always entered. Then she heard his step on the stair away down on the first flight, and she turned white for just a moment. She had a habit of saying little silent prayers about the simplest everyday things, and now she whispered: "Please, God, make him think I am still pretty."

The door opened and Jim stepped in and closed it. He looked thin and very serious. Poor fellow, he was only twenty-two—and to be burdened with a family! He needed a new overcoat and he was without gloves.

Jim stopped inside the door, as immovable as a setter at the scent of quail. His eyes were fixed upon Della, and there was an expression in them that she could not read, and it terrified her. It was not anger, nor surprise, nor disapproval, nor horror, nor any of the sentiments that she had been prepared for. He simply stared at her fixedly with that peculiar expression on his face.

Della wriggled off the table and went for him.

"Jim, darling," she cried, "don't look at me that way. I had my hair cut off and sold it because I couldn't have lived through Christmas without giving you a present. It'll grow again—you won't mind, will you? I just had to do it. My hair grows awfully fast. Say 'Merry Christmas!' Jim, and let's be happy. You don't know what a nice—what a beautiful, nice gift I've got for you."

"You've cut off your hair?" asked Jim, laboriously, as if he had not arrived at that patent fact yet even after the hardest mental labor.

"Cut it off and sold it," said Della. "Don't you like me just as well, anyhow? I'm me without my hair, ain't I?"

Jim looked about the room curiously.

"You say your hair is gone?" he said, with an air almost of idiocy.

"You needn't look for it," said Della. "It's sold, I tell you—sold and gone, too. It's Christmas Eve, boy. Be good to me, for it went for you. Maybe the hairs of my head were numbered," she went on with a sudden serious sweetness, "but nobody could ever count my love for you. Shall I put the chops on, Jim?"

Out of his trance Jim seemed to quickly wake. He enfolded his Della. For ten seconds let us regard with discreet scrutiny some inconsequential object in the other direction. Eight dollars a week or a million dollars a year—what is the difference? A mathematician or a wit would give you the wrong answer. The magi brought valuable gifts, but that was not among them. This dark assertion will be illuminated later on.

Jim drew a package from his overcoat pocket and threw it upon the table.

"Don't make any mistake, Dell," he said, "about me. I don't think there's anything in the way of a haircut or a shave or a shampoo that could make me like my girl any less. But if you'll unwrap that package you may see why you had me going awhile at first."

White fingers and nimble tore at the string and paper. And then an ecstatic scream of joy; and then alas a quick feminine change to hysterical tears and wails, necessitating the immediate employment of all the comforting powers of the lord of the flat.

For there lay The Combs—the set of combs, side and back, that Della had worshiped for long in a Broadway window. Beautiful combs, pure tortoise shell, with jewelled rims—just the shade to wear in the beautiful vanished hair. They were expensive combs, she knew, and her heart had simply craved and yearned over them without the least hope of possession. And now, they were hers, but the tresses that should have adorned the coveted adornments were gone.

But she hugged them to her bosom, and at length she was able to look up with dim eyes and a smile and say: "My hair grows so fast, Jim!"

And then Della leaped up like a little singed cat and cried, "Oh, oh!"

Jim had not yet seen his beautiful present. She held it out to him eagerly upon her open palm. The dull, precious metal seemed to flash with a reflection of her bright and ardent spirit.

"Isn't it a dandy, Jim? I hunted all over town to find it. You'll have to look at the time a hundred times a day now. Give me your watch. I want to see how it looks on it."

Instead of obeying, Jim tumbled down on the couch and put his hands under the back of his head and smiled.

"Dell," said he, "let's put our Christmas presents away and keep 'em a while. They're too nice to use just at present. I sold the watch to get money to buy your combs. And now suppose you put the chops on."

The magi, as you know, were wise men—wonderfully wise men—who brought gifts to the Babe in the manger. They invented the art of giving Christmas gifts. Being wise, their gifts were no doubt wise ones, possibly bearing the privilege of exchange in case of duplication. And here I have lamely related to you the uneventful chronicle of foolish children in a flat who most unwisely sacrificed for each other the greatest treasures of their house. But in a last word to the wise of these days let it be said that of all who give gifts these two were of the wisest. Of all who give and receive gifts, such as they are wisest. Everywhere they are wisest. They are the magi.

Christmas Is for Miracles

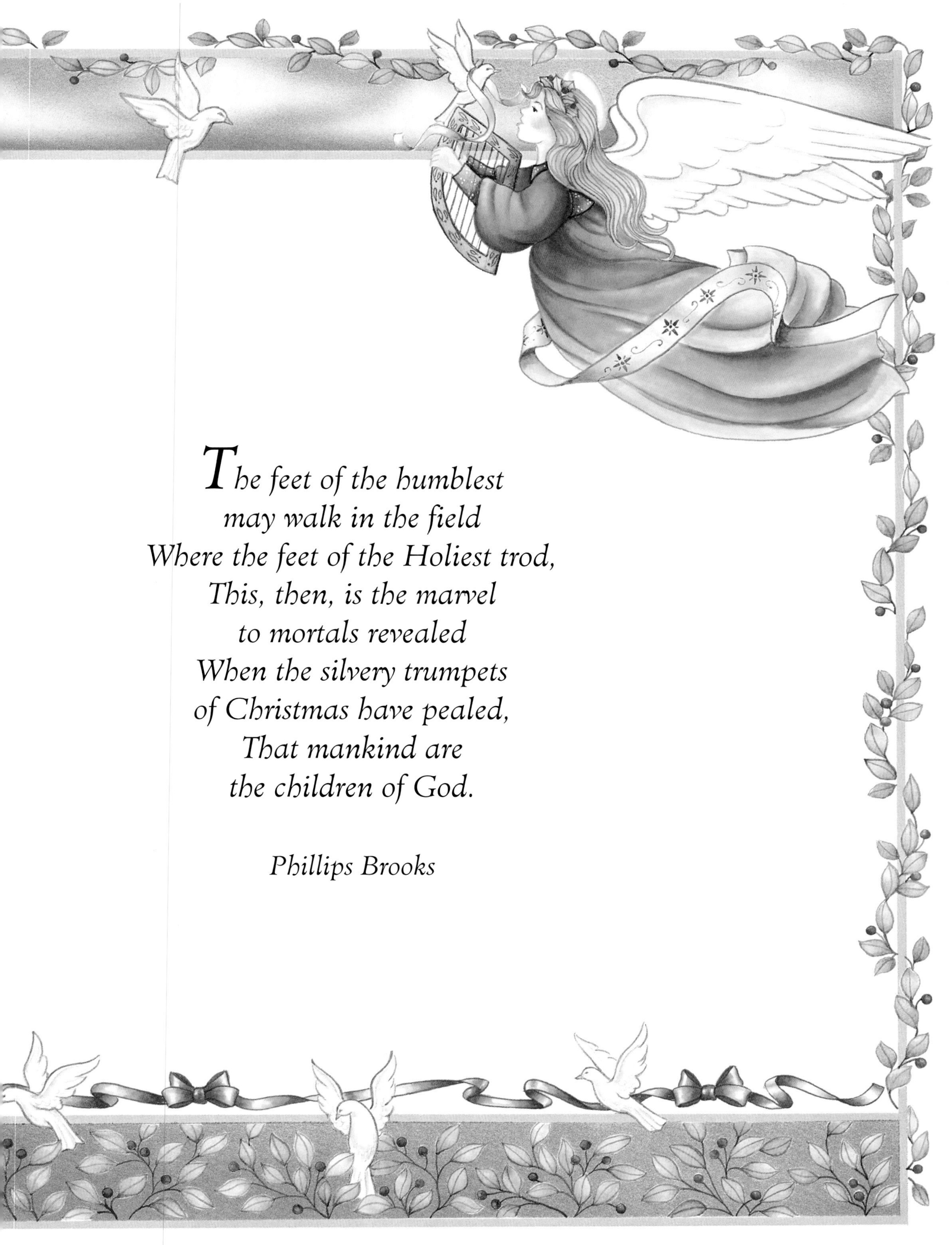

The feet of the humblest
may walk in the field
Where the feet of the Holiest trod,
This, then, is the marvel
to mortals revealed
When the silvery trumpets
of Christmas have pealed,
That mankind are
the children of God.

Phillips Brooks

The Last Name

Author Unknown

He who first wrote the name, wrote it at the end of the list—-below every name. He was a Roman officer, charged with the duty of the census in the district about Bethlehem. All day long the line of tired pilgrims had filed before the desk. At last the wearying record was completed: the officer set himself to reviewing the columns. Then suddenly a shadow fell across the page. He turned impatiently toward the doorway to see the figure of a stalwart man outlined against the setting sun, a child in his arms.

"I could not come earlier," he said, "the child was born last night."

"You are at the inn?" the officer asked.

"No, we arrived too late: the babe was born in a manger."

"Your name?"

"Joseph."

"Of what tribe?"

"The tribe of Benjamin and David. We are descendants of Kings," he added.

The officer did not look up. The world was full of the sons of former kings—and now there was no king but Caesar—lord of the earth by right of war.

"Your wife's name?"

"Mary."

"The baby's name?"

"Jesus."

The voice of the big man was soft, as though fondling the syllables.

"It means the Saviour of his people."

The officer merely nodded.

"Jesus, son of Joseph, of the tribe of Benjamin," he wrote and closed the book. It was the last name on the list.

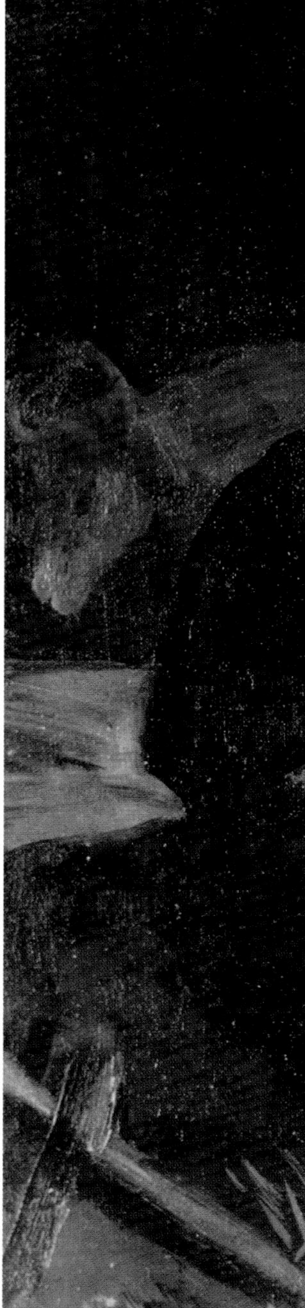

Adoration of the Shepherds
Robert Leinweber, 1845–1915

And It Came to Pass

Luke 2:1–18

And it came to pass in those days, that there went out a decree from Caesar Augustus, that all the world should be taxed. . . . And all went to be taxed, every one into his own city. And Joseph also went up from Galilee, out of the city of Nazareth, into Judaea, unto the city of David, which is called Bethlehem; (because he was of the house and lineage of David to be taxed with Mary his espoused wife, being great with child.

And so it was, that, while they were there, the days were accomplished that she should be delivered. And she brought forth her firstborn son, and wrapped him in swaddling clothes, and laid him in a manger; because there was no room for them in the inn.

And there were in the same country shepherds abiding in the field, keeping watch over their flock by night. And, lo, the angel of the Lord came upon them, and the glory of the Lord shone round about them: and they were sore afraid. And the angel said unto them, Fear not: for, behold, I bring you good tidings of great joy, which shall be to all people. For unto you is born this day in the city of David a Saviour, which is Christ the Lord.

And this shall be a sign unto you; Ye shall find the babe wrapped in swaddling clothes, lying in a manger. And suddenly there was with the angel a multitude of the heavenly host praising God, and saying, Glory to God in the highest, and on earth peace, good will toward men.

And it came to pass, as the angels were gone away from them into heaven, the shepherds said one to another, Let us now go even unto Bethlehem, and see this thing which is come to pass, which the Lord hath made known unto us. And they came with haste, and found Mary, and Joseph, and the babe lying in a manger. And when they had seen it, they made known abroad the saying which was told them concerning this child. And all they that heard it wondered at those things which were told them by the shepherds.

Adoration of the Magi
Camillo Procaccini, 1560–1629

Angels

Billy Graham

Dr. S. W. Mitchell, a celebrated Philadelphia neurologist, had gone to bed after an exceptionally tiring day. Suddenly he was awakened by someone knocking on his door. Opening it he found a little girl, poorly dressed and deeply upset. She told him her mother was very sick and asked him if he would please come with her. It was a bitterly cold, snowy night, but though he was bone tired, Dr. Mitchell dressed and followed the girl.

He found the mother desperately ill with pneumonia. After arranging for medical care, he complimented the sick woman on the intelligence and persistence of her little daughter. The woman looked at him strangely and then said, "My daughter died a month ago." She added, "Her shoes and coat are in the clothes closet there." Dr. Mitchell, amazed and perplexed, went to the closet and opened the door. There hung the very coat worn by the little girl who had brought him to tend to her mother. It was warm and dry and could not possibly have been out in the wintry night.

The Reverend John G. Paton, a missionary in the New Hebrides Islands, tells a thrilling story involving the protective care of angels. Hostile natives surrounded his mission headquarters one night, intent on burning the Patons out and killing them. John Paton and his wife prayed all during that terror-filled night that God would deliver them. When daylight came they were amazed to see the attackers unaccountably leave. They thanked God for delivering them.

A year later, the chief of the tribe was converted to Christianity, and Mr. Paton, remembering what had happened, asked the chief what had kept him and his men from burning down the house and killing them. The chief replied in surprise, "Who were all those men you had with you there?" The missionary answered, "There were no men there; just my wife and I." The chief argued that they had seen many men standing guard—hundreds of big men in shining garments with drawn swords in their hands. They seemed to circle the mission station so that the natives were afraid to attack. Only then did Mr. Paton realize that God had sent His angels to protect them. The chief agreed that there was no other explanation.

During World War II, Captain Eddie Rickenbacker was shot down over the Pacific Ocean. For weeks nothing was heard of him. The newspapers reported his disappearance and across the country thousands of people prayed. Mayor LaGuardia asked the whole city of New York to pray for him.

Then he returned. The Sunday papers headlined the news, and in an article, Captain Rickenbacker himself told what had happened. "And this part I would hesitate to tell," he wrote, "except that there were six witnesses who saw it with me.

"A gull came out of nowhere, and lighted on my head. I reached up my hand very gently. I killed him and then we divided him equally among us. We ate every bit, even the little bones. Nothing ever tasted so good." This gull saved the lives of Rickenbacker and his companions.

Years later I asked him to tell me the story personally, because it was through this experience that he came to know Christ. He said, "I have no explanation except that God sent one of His angels to rescue us. . . ."

Does it not seem mysterious that God brought the first message of the birth of Jesus to ordinary people rather than to princes and kings? In this instance, God spoke through His holy angel to the shepherds who were keeping sheep in the fields. This was a lowly occupation, so shepherds were not well educated. But Mary in her song, the Magnificat, tells us the true story: "He hath put down the mighty from their seats, and exalted them of low degree. He hath filled the hungry with good things; and the rich he hath sent empty away" (Luke 1:52–53).

What a word for our generation!

What was the message of the angel to the shepherds? First, he told them not to be afraid. Over and over again the presence of angels was frightening to those to whom they came. But unless they came in judgment, the angels spoke a word of reassurance. They calmed the people to whom they came. This tells us that the appearance of an angel is awe-inspiring, something about them awakening fear in the human heart. They represent a presence that has greatness and sends a chill down the spine. But when the angel had quieted the fears of the shepherds, he brought this message, one forever to be connected with the angel:

"For, behold, I bring you good tidings of great joy, which shall be to all people. For unto you is born this day in the city of David a Saviour, which is Christ the Lord."

Joy Attend Your Yuletide
Unknown Nineteenth- or Twentieth-Century Artist

A Christmas Carol

Sara Teasdale

The kings they came from out the south,
All dressed in ermine fine;
They bore Him gold and chrysoprase,
And gifts of precious wine.

The shepherds came from out the north,
Their coats were brown and old;
They brought Him little newborn lambs—
They had not any gold.

The wise men came from out the east,
And they were wrapped in white;
The star that led them all the way
Did glorify the night.

The angels came from heaven high,
And they were clad with wings;
And lo, they brought a joyful song
The host of heaven sings.

The kings they knocked upon the door,
The wise men entered in,
The shepherds followed after them
To hear the song begin.

The angels sang through all the night
Until the rising sun,
But little Jesus fell asleep
Before the song was done.

Adoration of the Magi
Hans Memling, 1433–1494

The Christmas Guest

Clarence Hawkes

He came and stood before the great front door,
In angry words they bade him go away.
He passed from sight, they saw his form no more,
For they were busy, as 'twas Christmas day.
At eve he sought another door instead,
And asked the servants for a bit of bread.

Most graciously they bade him come inside,
And spread a goodly meal of bread and meat,
And as he ate appraisingly they eyed,
His face and form, e'en to his hands and feet.
They knew not whom they entertained that night,
His voice was kind, his face was full of light.

"This is a goodly house," he said, "and fair,
Yet something lacks of kindliness and joy."
"It is the very dungeon of despair,"
A servant said, "and all its gold alloy,
For love's not here, but arrogance and pride,
Where love is lost there's nothing else beside."

'Tis so," he said, "I know such people well,
In days of old they called them Pharisees,
Of all their pomp and power they love to tell,
I saw them oft across the seven seas.
A blessing on this house I freely give,
May they forget their gold and learn to live."

Awhile he spoke, the room was full of light,
And in each heart there came a wondrous peace.
These servants poor had fed the Lord that night,
And he had caused their doubts and fears to cease.
Thus oft He seeks in vain the palace door,
But sups in humble homes where men adore.

Heaven Cannot Hold Him

Christina Rossetti

In the bleak midwinter
Frosty wind made moan,
Earth stood hard as iron,
Water like a stone;
Snow had fallen, snow on snow,
Snow on snow,
In the bleak midwinter
Long ago.

Our God, Heaven cannot hold Him
Nor earth sustain;
Heaven and earth shall flee away
When He comes to reign:
In the bleak midwinter
A stable-place sufficed
The Lord God Almighty
Jesus Christ.

Angels and archangels
May have gathered there,
Cherubim and seraphim
Thronged the air;
But only His mother
In her maiden bliss
Worshiped the Beloved
With a kiss.

Enough for Him, whom cherubim
Worship night and day,
A breastful of milk
And a mangerful of hay;
Enough for Him, whom angels
Fall down before,
The ox and ass and camel
Which adore.

What can I give Him,
Poor as I am?
If I were a shepherd
I would bring a lamb,
If I were a Wise Man
I would do my part—
Yet what I can I give Him,
Give my heart.

A Christmas Carol

Christina Rossetti

Before the paling of the stars,
Before the winter morn,
Before the earliest cockcrow,
Jesus Christ was born;
Born in a stable,
Cradled in a manger,
In the world His hands had made,
Born a stranger.

Priest and king lay fast asleep
In Jerusalem,
Young and old lay fast asleep
In crowded Bethlehem;

Saint and angel, ox and ass
Kept a watch together,
Before the Christmas daybreak
In the winter weather.

Jesus on His Mother's breast,
In the stable cold,
Spotless Lamb of God was He,
Shepherd of the fold:
Let us kneel with Mary Maid,
With Joseph bent and hoary,
With saint and angel, ox and ass,
To hail the King of glory.

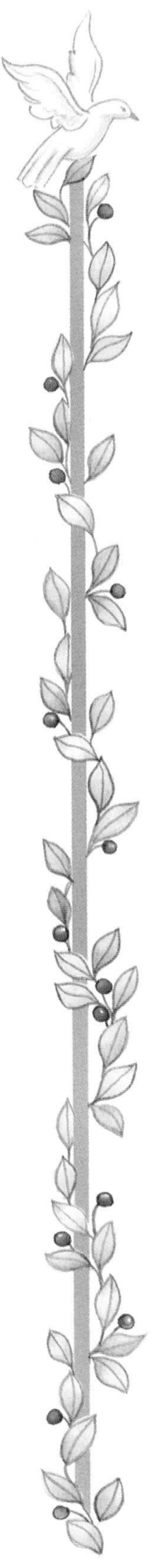

Christmas Day in the Morning

Pearl S. Buck

He woke suddenly and completely. It was four o'clock, the hour at which his father had always called him to get up and help with the milking. Strange how the habits of his youth clung to him still! Fifty years ago, and his father had been dead for thirty years, and yet he waked at four o'clock in the morning. He had trained himself to turn over and go to sleep, but this morning, because it was Christmas, he did not try to sleep.

Yet what was the magic of Christmas now? His childhood and youth were long past, and his own children had grown up and gone. Some of them lived only a few miles away but they had their own families, and though they would come in as usual toward the end of the day, they had explained with infinite gentleness that they wanted their children to build Christmas memories about their houses, not his. He was left alone with his wife.

Yesterday she had said, "It isn't worthwhile, perhaps—"

And he had said, "Oh, yes, Alice, even if there are only the two of us, let's have a Christmas of our own."

Then she had said, "Let's not trim the tree until tomorrow, Robert—just so it's ready when the children come. I'm tired."

He had agreed, and the tree was still out in the back entry.

He lay in his big bed in his room. The door to her room was shut because she was a light sleeper, and sometimes he had restless nights. Years ago they had decided to use separate rooms. It meant nothing, they said, except that neither of them slept as well as they once had. They had been married so long that nothing could separate them, actually.

Why did he feel so awake tonight? For it was still night, a clear and starry night. No moon, of course, but the stars were extraordinary! Now that he thought of it, the stars seemed always large and clear before the dawn of Christmas Day. There was one star now that was certainly larger and brighter than any of the others. He could even imagine it moving, as it had seemed to him to move one night long ago.

He slipped back in time, as he did so easily nowadays. He was fifteen years old and still on his father's farm. He loved his father. He had not known it until one day a few days before Christmas, when he had overheard what his father was saying to his mother.

"Mary, I hate to call Rob in the mornings. He's growing so fast and he needs his sleep. If you could see how he sleeps when I go in to wake him up! I wish I could manage alone."

"Well, you can't, Adam." His mother's voice was brisk. "Besides, he isn't a child anymore. It's time he took his turn."

"Yes," his father said slowly. "But I sure do hate to wake him."

When he heard these words, something in him woke: his father loved him! He had never thought of it before, taking for granted the tie of their blood. Neither his father nor his mother talked about loving their children—they had no time for such things. There was always so much to do on a farm.

Now that he knew his father loved him, there would be no more loitering in the mornings and having to be called again. He got up after that, stumbling blind with sleep, and pulled on his clothes, his eyes tight shut, but he got up.

And then on the night before Christmas, that year when he was fifteen, he lay for a few minutes thinking about the next day. They were poor, and most of the excitement was in the turkey they had raised themselves and in the mince pies his mother made. His sisters sewed presents and his mother and father always bought something he needed, not only a warm jacket, maybe, but something more, such as a book. And he saved and bought them each something, too.

He wished, that Christmas he was fifteen, he had a better present for his father. As usual he had gone to the ten-cent store and bought a tie. It had seemed nice enough until he lay thinking the night before Christmas, and then he wished that he had heard his father and mother talking in time for him to save for something better.

He lay on his side, his head supported by his elbow, and looked out of his attic window. The stars were bright, much brighter than he ever remembered seeing them, and one star in particular was so bright that he wondered if it were really the Star of Bethlehem.

"Dad," he had once asked when he was a little boy, "what is a stable?"

"It's just a barn," his father had replied, "like ours."

Then Jesus had been born in a barn, and to a barn the shepherds and the Wise Men had come, bringing their Christmas gifts!

The thought struck him like a silver dagger. Why should he not give his father a special gift too, out there in the barn? He could get up early, earlier than four o'clock, and he could creep into the barn and get all the milking done. He'd do it alone, milk and clean up, and then when his father went in to start the milking, he'd see it all done. And he would know who had done it.

He laughed to himself as he gazed at the stars. It was what he would do, and he mustn't sleep too sound.

He must have waked twenty times, scratching a match each time to look at his old watch—midnight, and half past one, and then two o'clock.

At a quarter to three he got up and put on his clothes. He crept downstairs, careful of the creaky boards, and let himself out. The big star hung lower over the barn roof, a reddish gold. The cows looked at him, sleepy and surprised. It was early for them, too.

"So, boss," he whispered. They accepted him placidly, and he fetched some hay for each cow and then got the milking pail and the big milk cans.

He had never milked all alone before, but it seemed almost easy. He kept thinking about his father's surprise. His father would come in and call him, saying that he would get things started while Rob was getting dressed. He'd go to the barn, open the door, and then he'd go to get the two big empty milk cans. But they wouldn't be waiting or empty; they'd be standing in the milkhouse, filled.

"What the—" he could hear his father exclaiming.

He smiled and milked steadily, two strong streams rushing into the pail, frothing and fragrant. The cows were still surprised but acquiescent. For once they were behaving well, as though they knew it was Christmas.

The task went more easily than he had ever known it to before. Milking for once was not a chore. It was something else, a gift to his father who loved him. He finished, the two milk cans were full, and he covered them and closed the milkhouse door carefully, making sure of the latch. He put the stool in its place by the door and hung up the clean milk pail. Then he went out of the barn and barred the door behind him.

Back in his room he had only a minute to pull off his clothes in the darkness and jump into bed, for he heard his father up. He put the covers over his head to silence his quick breathing. The door opened.

"Rob!" his father called "We have to get up, son, even if it is Christmas."

"Aw-right," he said sleepily.

"I'll go on out," his father said. "I'll get things started."

The door closed and he lay still, laughing to himself. In just a few minutes his father would know. His dancing heart was ready to jump from his body.

The minutes were endless—ten, fifteen, he did not know how many—and he heard his father's footsteps again. The door opened and he lay still.

"Rob!"

"Yes, Dad—"

His father was laughing, a queer sobbing sort of a laugh. "Thought you'd fool me, did you?" His father was standing beside his bed, feeling for him, pulling away the cover.

"It's for Christmas, Dad!"

He found his father and clutched him in a great hug. He felt his father's arms go around him. It was dark and they could not see each other's faces.

"Son, I thank you. Nobody ever did a nicer thing—"

"Oh, Dad, I want you to know—I do want to be good!" The words broke from him of their own will. He did not know what to say. His heart was bursting with love.

"Well, I reckon I can go back to bed and sleep," his father said after a moment. "No, hark—the little ones are waked up. Come to think of it, son, I've never seen you children when you first saw the Christmas tree. I was always in the barn. Come on!"

He got up and pulled on his clothes again and they went down to the Christmas tree, and soon the sun was creeping up to where the star had been. Oh, what a Christmas, and how his heart had nearly burst again with shyness and pride as his father told his mother and made the younger children listen about how he, Rob, had got up all by himself.

"The best Christmas gift I ever had, and I'll remember it, son, every year on Christmas morning, so long as I live."

They had both remembered it, and now that his father was dead he remembered it alone: that blessed Christmas dawn when, alone with the cows in the barn, he had made his first gift of true love.

Outside the window now the great star slowly sank. He got up out of bed

and put on his slippers and bathrobe and went softly upstairs to the attic and found the box of Christmas-tree decorations. He took them downstairs into the living room. Then he brought in the tree. It was a little one—they had not had a big tree since the children went away—but he set it in the holder and put it in the middle of the long table under the window. Then carefully he began to trim it. It was done very soon, the time passing as quickly as it had that morning long ago in the barn.

He went to his library and fetched the little box that contained his special gift to his wife, a star of diamonds, not large but dainty in design. He had written the card for it the day before. He tied the gift on the tree and then stood back. It was pretty, very pretty, and she would be surprised.

But he was not satisfied. He wanted to tell her—to tell her how much he loved her. It had been a long time since he had really told her, although he loved her in a very special way, much more than he ever had when they were young.

He had been fortunate that she had loved him—and how fortunate that he had been able to love! Ah, that was the true joy of life, the ability to love! For he was quite sure that some people were genuinely unable to love anyone. But love was alive in him, it still was.

It occurred to him suddenly that it was alive because long ago it had been born in him when he knew his father loved him. That was it: love alone could waken love.

And he could give the gift again and again. This morning, this blessed Christmas morning, he would give it to his beloved wife. He could write it down in a letter for her to read and keep forever. He went to his desk and began his love letter to his wife: My dearest love. . . .

When it was finished he sealed it and tied it on the tree where she would see it the first thing when she came into the room. She would read it, surprised and then moved, and realize how very much he loved her.

He put out the light and went tiptoeing up the stairs. The star in the sky was gone, and the first rays of the sun were gleaming the sky. Such a happy, happy Christmas!

"Every good gift and every perfect gift is from above, and cometh down from the Father of lights, with whom is no variableness, neither shadow of turning."

James 1:17

Antique Austrian Christmas Decorations

A Christmas Carol

G. K. Chesterton

The Christ-child lay on Mary's lap,
His hair was like a light,
(O weary, weary were the world,
But here is all aright.)

The Christ-child lay on Mary's breast,
His hair was like a star.
(O stern and cunning are the kings,
But here the true hearts are.)

The Christ-child lay on Mary's heart,
His hair was like a fire.
(O weary, weary is the world,
But here the world's desire.)

The Christ-child stood at Mary's knee,
His hair was like a crown,
And all the flowers looked up at him
And all the stars looked down.

"Therefore the Lord himself
shall give you a sign;
Behold, a virgin shall conceive,
and bear a son, and shall call
his name Immanuel."
Isaiah 7:14

The Oxen

Thomas Hardy

Christmas Eve, and twelve of the clock.
"Now they are all on their knees,"
An elder said as we sat in a flock
By the embers in hearthside ease.

We pictured the meek mild creatures where
They dwelt in their strawy pen,
Nor did it occur to one of us there
To doubt they were kneeling then.

So fair a fancy few would weave
In these years! Yet, I feel
If someone said on Christmas Eve,
"Come see the oxen kneel
In the lonely barton by yonder coomb
Our childhood used to know,"
I should go with him in the gloom,
Hoping it might be so.

Red Barn under Christmas Snow
Litchfield, Connecticut

A Christmas Prayer

Peter Marshall

In a world that seems not only to be changing, but even to be dissolving,
there are some tens of millions of us who want Christmas to be the same . . .
with the same old greeting "Merry Christmas" and no other.

We long for the abiding love among men of good will
which the season brings . . . believing in this ancient miracle of Christmas
with its softening, sweetening influence to tug at our heart strings once again.

We want to hold on to the old customs and traditions because
they strengthen our family ties, bind us to our friends,
make us one with all mankind for whom the Child was born,
and bring us back again to the God Who gave His only begotten
Son, that "Whosoever believeth in Him should not perish,
but have everlasting life."

So we will not "spend" Christmas . . . nor "observe" Christmas.
We will "keep" Christmas—keep it as it is . . . in all the loveliness
of its ancient traditions.

May we keep it in our hearts, that we may be kept in its hope.

Country Christmas Living Room

Index by Author

A B C D E F G H I J
1 2 3 4 5 6 7 8 9 0